Soul Passion

Embracing Your Life's
Ultimate Purpose

THE INTENTIONAL LIFE TRILOGY

BOOK ONE

Soul Passion

Embracing Your Life's

Ultimate Purpose

Ramesh Richard

MOODY PUBLISHERS
CHICAGO

Produced with the assistance of The Livingstone Corporation (www.LivingstoneCorp.com). Project staff includes Mary Horner Collins, Kirk Luttrell, Ashley Taylor, and Neil Wilson.

ISBN 0-8024-6460-2

1 3 5 7 9 10 8 6 4 2

Printed in the United States of America

To friend, mentor, and advocate
Fred Smith Sr.

Four decades of chronological distance
disappear each time we meet.

At a hundred lunches of one-way benefit,
he has nurtured me in wisdom and courage.

Contents

Introduction

Welcome to *Soul Passion,* Book One of the Intentional Life Trilogy, a three-volume blueprint for building and living a purposeful, meaningful, and useful life. Building a house or a life requires envisioning, planning, and implementation. Your life provides an immediate and astounding opportunity to build a powerful, beautiful, and worthwhile future, beginning now.

This series on restructuring life from randomness to intentionality comes in three larger sections: *Passion, Mission,* and *Vision.* Each segment contains a prologue, continues explanation with illustration, and calls for a personal response. I invite you to read these books slowly, twice. First, read with a pen. Use the margins. Interact with me, understand the arguments, predict and critique me. If you find the book helpful, read it second time with a notebook open. Dialogue with God. Write out your thoughts. In that reflection, you'll find a reservoir of resources for building and living the intentional life

Soul Passion will benefit you in two ways-in preparing the "site" and in laying the foundation for the Intentional Life. Once the foundation is in place, you will be ready for Book Two, *Soul Mission,* which shows the way to utilize the space above the foundation, in designing, dividing, and developing the "first floor" of your life. After that, Book Three, *Soul Vision,* describes the height to which you implement God's vision and your aspiration in this new way of living. Together, these volumes will help you understand and realize the grand, divine narrative for your life.

Be prepared for a jarring beginning. The first three chapters cover preliminary and literal groundbreaking work-site preparation. These chapters could feel a little like a wrecking crew has descended on you. Heavy equipment will rumble and the dirt may fly. Some of your cherished assumptions of life are about to be splintered. Some of your unexamined behaviors are about to be upturned. Some of your attitudes are about to be carried away to the landfill. But that's what it takes to build a life-clearing away of the debris and the rubble of an Unintentional Life, accumulated over time through senseless busyness and with useless stuff.

Get ready for a serious project. I sincerely hope that you are prepared to undertake a radical examination and yield to a total renovation of your life. The hours you spend reading and thinking (and possibly praying) about the content in these books will generate echoes in eternity. Let the Intentional Life begin!

"Gone to the Dogs!"

Too many human beings live unintentionally. You may be among them. You *unintentionally* live unintentionally.[1] The best example I know to illustrate the unintentional life isn't human. He is consistent, recognizable, and will not take offense in illustrating the unintentional life. Let me introduce you to Fudge, our extremely rare breed Nova Scotia Retriever look-alike. He lives the unintentional life with abandon. In fact, Fudge's daily routine bears uncanny resemblance to the typical human life. He may just be your canine clone.

> *Maybe in order to understand mankind we have to look at the word itself. MANKIND. Basically, it's made up of two separate words, "mank" and "ind." What do these words mean? It's a mystery and that's why so is mankind.*
>
> *DEEP THOUGHTS,*
> JACK HANDEY

THE UNINTENTIONAL LIFE MAKES NOISE

Fudge makes noise. He's infamous for his racket in our neighborhood—especially his piercing, midnight howl. He rudely and randomly wakes everyone up to get our attention, content even to be reprimanded. His self-focused barking cries for immediate response. Once I turn on the patio lights, he feels wanted for the rest of the night.

People make noises, too. Their existence is readily acknowledged in their minor spheres of near-sovereign influence. Some only get noticed within their sub-subcultures, but that attention is enough to prime their pump. For too many of us, life consists in getting noticed. We keep going as long as someone pays attention.

Take sports megastars for instance. Cultures and games may vary, but when sports heroes make noise, everyone listens. In Indonesia, a badminton champion plays the role of trendsetter. Pakistan once featured Imran Khan, a world-class cricket player. When he made noise, a nation woke up to turn on the lights for him. Though less and less, the whole world still recognizes Michael Jordan, arguably history's greatest basketball player. The world adopts his athletic shoe preference, the breakfast cereal he eats, the soft drinks he imbibes, and the phone company he promotes. When Jordan barks, people hurry to buy what he barks' about. But advertising clout doesn't last. Today's rising stars are tomorrow's falling stars. Culture will attempt to immortalize them in halls of fame, but they will soon fade to faint and fuzzy memories for most people. Presumably, that's what fierce, street fighter turned champion boxer Mike Tyson, realized after a loss in 2002. When asked about his future, he replied, "I guess I'm going to fade into Bolivian."

Oblivion, our forced vacation destination, offers us no genuine choices. We make noise during seasons of temporary prominence, but time stalks us. Death overcomes the best of us. Our barks get muffled with age, and we finally turn mute.

No one escapes. The more conspicuous the stage, be it music, politics, business, the professions, cinema, religion, sports, or science, the more obvious the oblivion-boundedness. The best known faces will eventually reside in the memory of a few, who themselves will soon become memories, till the curtain falls. It inevitably gets dark and silent. No one hears their barks anymore.

Yelp, yip, or yap softly—you can't make as impressive a noise as the rich, powerful, and famous, but you do make noise in your world. It may be in your marriage, your home, your business, or on your campus. Sometimes you snarl or growl, but mostly you just bark. Those who want to make you feel wanted turn on the porch lights. With a little attention, your loneliness subsides. Your hurt is dulled. Someone *does* seem to care enough to notice you. But the encroaching darkness presses a question: will the attention outlast your brief flicker on the swiftly changing, high-definition screen of biology and history?

Yes, you need to bark. The question, though, is, are you barking for a purpose, with a purpose? Are you barking for vague, canine-like instincts, or for a reason? Is the volume, the loudness of your bark, related to your purpose for barking? Remember that once people get used to your dogness, they'll start taking your bark lightly. Don't bark too much, or you will have to resort to biting in order to get attention. You know what they do to dogs that bite.

Fudge demonstrates that making noise doesn't make you human. Making *intentional* noise, intelligible noise, to accomplish a purpose qualifies you for the appellation "human." A message on our Dallas basketball arena's jumbotron frequently summons the crowd with "JUST MAKE NOISE." The audience yells wildly, yet our team often plays mildly. What would you think if the message came on, the crowd erupted, the rafters shook, but there was no game to play, the court empty since no players showed up? You'd think that was wasted noise. Purposeless noisemaking is a waste of energy, of life itself.

Does your noisemaking follow a purpose? A worthy purpose? A lofty purpose? Or is it simply the sound of an unintentional life?

THE UNINTENTIONAL LIFE RUNS IN CIRCLES

Fudge must run. A speed demon when kids are present, he whizzes by them. They chase him. He stops for a moment. Just when they reach him, he blasts off to another corner of the backyard. The kids finally get there. Again he escapes, playfully teasing them. He and the kids have a good time. But they never touch him.

You are like that, too. Caught in a blur of activity, you are so busy you should quit. But you don't plan for reflection or find time to mourn over your busyness. Each morning the race continues at full speed. No time to peruse the newspaper leisurely, you glance worriedly at the business pages—how did your investments perform yesterday? A Hong Kong stockbroker-friend sleeps with cell phone, television, e-mail, and fax machine on, ready to ring, buzz, or whine next to his bed as he manages funds worldwide. Between New York, Tokyo, Zurich, and Singapore markets, someone's doing business around the clock. A speed demon of a man, he keeps up with the pace of a 24-hour global economy but drives his family crazy. He whizzes by them. Finally, just as his children reach him, information from the marketplace interrupts, requiring an urgent decision. He blasts off to another emotional corner. He has a good time. Of course, his kids don't get to touch him.

What's he running around for? Why is he so busy? Is it really worth it?

By the way, Fudge also runs in circles. Especially if he is chained to the live oak in our yard. He can't get anywhere, but he dashes around, fast, furious, until he gets tangled tightly around the tree. We are afraid he'll choke himself because he doesn't think to turn around. He can't help himself. Our son Robby has to unchain him, free him from the outside. I'm afraid for you, too. I don't want you to choke yourself. Perhaps help from a compassionate master will unshackle you.[2]

THE UNINTENTIONAL LIFE FOCUSES ON EXTERNALS

Most who see Fudge immediately acknowledge his good looks. He's quite huggable. He's got a cute face and nice proportions. He could easily carry the cover of *Dogue*. Our teenagers would settle for the inside back cover of *Gentlehound's Quarterly* for the right fee.

He wears the finest outfit a dog could wear—that's where he gets his name—draped in shiny chocolate brown. Of course, he doesn't know he's dressed elegantly. But people notice his impressive appearance and charm. Fudge possesses everything—personality, looks, attire—everything. Wow! Bow-wow!

An obstetrician friend once boasted the second-biggest solo practice in Houston, America's fourth-largest city. Averaging ninety cases a day, he prided himself in going ten months without a day off, seven days a week. He met every goal he set for himself before turning the age of forty. He was particularly known for his exterior—his wardrobe, his wife's accouterments, his estate, private plane, and vacation home (rarely used). He met me at the airport in his brand new, bright red, road-hugging, road-skimming, road-gliding Porsche. "I've been putting on the dog," he guiltily confided. In the throes of divorce, he finally began asking the right human question: Why am I doing this? He eventually stopped imitating my dog. His wife became more than a doll to dress up. The questions that drove him beyond canine compulsion were noble: What's my show for? Why am I running so fast, working so hard, dressed up so well? What am I hiding in my busyness? What is the goal and purpose of my life?

Noble questions, however noble they are, don't come with answers built into them. Not knowing what else to do, he continued to work his tail off. Decked out on the outside, empty on the inside. "Putting on the dog"—what an apt metaphor! Shouldn't there be some purpose to dressing well, looking sharp, working hard, making money, and evoking compliments from half-jealous peers?

THE UNINTENTIONAL LIFE LIVES TO CONSUME

You knew I'd come to canine eating habits. Fudge practices consumption bordering on food inhalation. Hungry or not, he devours most food with voracious passion. He loves snacking between feasts. He salivates watching the kids get his food ready. Occasionally he rejects a meal for no discernible reason. He relishes a chewable bonus, an occasional reward, for unintentionally being a dog.

When I was growing up in southern India, my family finished each meal with a discussion about the next one. Partly driven by economic uncertainties, we mused, is there going to be another meal, and a hearty one at that? Food availability wasn't the only obstacle. Without prepackaging, microwaves, or refrigeration, meal preparation for our extended family was complicated. So, plans for our next meal often consumed our enjoyment of the present one.

Our family tradition continues, though the economics of procuring and preparing meals have changed. I found that the fine food orientation certainly exists beyond our family. A couple "confessed" that for years they simply lived to eat. They elaborately planned food forays, choosing from an array of restaurants, calling in reservations, making friends with chefs who might create delectable platters for discriminating appetites. And then, before the meal was over, they would blissfully anticipate the one to follow. Between meals they consumed snacks. Or better, between snacks all they had to eat was breakfast, lunch, and dinner.

Is the human condition about cuisine and clothing, or is life more than food and raiment? Should we live to eat as life's purpose, or eat to live as food's purpose? My alarm just beeped. It's lunchtime. An important appointment determines that I will probably also eat. Would I order food if there were no engagement? Should I eat even if I'm not hungry?

THE UNINTENTIONAL LIFE
PLEASES ITSELF

Dogs run after the next pleasure, the next pleaser. "Self-pleasing," Fudge's first principle, controls his daily conduct. Easily enticed by female callers, he forgoes social etiquette in approaching his guest. No reserve to overcome, no distance to bridge, no social or moral barriers to discuss. Attracted and aroused, he only knows one way to meet a stranger. When the female departs, Fudge offers no farewell and feels no remorse. Appetite satisfied, pleasure obtained, life is full, until another playmate is available.

Each Monday morning in Miami, two thousand passengers file off the *MS Ecstasy*, a 70,000-ton Carnival Cruise Line ship that towers thirteen stories above the quay. Later in the day the next two thousand passengers will pile aboard, to make way four days later for another group, who in turn will switch with another group the following Monday. Where are they sailing? No "where." It doesn't matter. "The 'Fun Ship' is not a means to an end. It is the destination!"[3] Cruises may be OK for a week or two. But if all of life resembles a fun ship, self becomes the ultimate purpose in life.

In the middle of 1995, approximately 731 current books contained the word "Self" in the title. Two had to do with *self-denial,* and they went quickly from publication to out-of-print status. The rest flew off the shelves, for they dealt with helping, pleasing, even aggrandizing one's Self. In narcissism, the self becomes the arbiter of life's quality, ethics, and passion. One's purpose for existence is the satisfaction of self. In creative and ludicrous expressions, society's mission in life is reduced to one ultimate—*self—my Self*. Crafting a purpose statement for personal life becomes easy: "I exist . . . for myself."

➤ *My* pleasures please me. Except my preferences change, and I lose interest.

➤ *My* passions persuade me. Only they are not sustainable in the long term.

➤ *My* principles pull me. Principles which I think are good for me by my criteria are absolutely good for living my life at any given moment of my unintentional, random existence.

➤ *My* people perform for me. I relate to them only as they are useful to me.

➤ I exist . . . to please *myself.*

A CHOICE TO MAKE

Since the behaviors we've discussed favor our lovable, family mongrel, is Fudge possibly a disguised human? Or is it simply that your life resembles and replicates selfish animal existence—the tolerably good life of a domesticated jackal?

If you bark for human attention, furiously run circles in daily activity, enjoy your own hugability, live to consume, and exist to please yourself, you've gone to the dogs. You are caught in a chain around the oak tree and in danger of choking. You may not even be able to bark. You need Someone from outside to untangle and untie you. Someone who sees your predicament and is willing to loosen the chain and set you free from the tree.

The parallels between animals and humans highlight the crucial value of an intentional life.[4] Your life deserves a purposeful existence. There are, as we will see, unworthy and worthy purposes, invalid and valid aims, small and large goals, but the presence of a purpose gives human life an "about-ness" that is not recognizable in mere animal life. That's the principle of intentionality. You must choose between randomly rambling through life and passionately living a purposeful life.

To go about life randomly and unintentionally is

➤ metaphorically, barking up the wrong tree;

➤ literally, a busyness that is "full of fury, signifying nothing";

➤ spiritually, a bubble existence fondled by acceptance,

fattened by consumption, and blown around by the whims of pleasure.

To go about life purposefully and intentionally is to be

➢ barking with content and meaning;

➢ busy with impact;

➢ buoyed with energy, direction, and balance.

This reflective book (and the two future companion volumes) offers insights to help prevent you from mimicking animal randomness. You'll only exhibit loose bio-syntactical connections with the lower animal kingdom. Don't go to the dogs.[5]

An Unintentional Life

Many wise people believe that the fundamental problem of the human race is purposelessness. That the persistent, basal question each person longs to answer is simply, "Why do I exist?"

I agree. Despite time, culture, or privilege, in ancient Athens or contemporary Singapore, in cultured opera houses or at pounding music concerts, forms of the existential "why" question haunt the human psyche.

"What is the purpose of life, *my life?* What is the point of it all?" All people intuitively ask that question. And they all answer it in some way, even when they don't think or know they are

> *Into the Universe, and*
> *Why not knowing*
> *Nor whence, like Water*
> *willy-nilly flowing*
> *And out of it, as Wind*
> *along the Waste*
> *I know not Whither,*
> *willy-nilly blowing.*
> — OMAR KHAYYAM

answering it. Some regret the busy, random activity of life toward the end of its duration. Others are vaguely unhappy with their answer, but they're not sure why. British literateur, publisher, and political activist Leonard Woolf, best known for editing his brilliant wife's (Virginia Woolf) writings, made a statement in his latter years that you need to read slowly:

> I see clearly that I have achieved practically nothing. The world today and the history of the human anthill during the past five to seven years would be exactly the same if I had played Ping-Pong instead of sitting on committees and writing books and memoranda. I have therefore to make a rather ignominious confession that I have in a long life ground through between 150,000 and 200,000 hours of perfectly useless work.[1]

NO PURPOSE

Serious thinkers have judged the "purpose" or "meaning" question as unanswerable. "There is really no purpose for your life as an individual" they hold. More popular summaries of purposelessness include:

> ➤ "The meaning of life is written inside the fortune cookie, and the slip is blank." (Susan Fromberg Schaeffer)

> ➤ "If you are not confused, you don't understand the situation." (bumper sticker)

> ➤ "Life is a jigsaw puzzle with most of the pieces missing."

> ➤ "Life is a riddle, wrapped in a mystery, inside a trauma." (borrowed from Winston Churchill's comment about Russia)

> ➤ "Life is solitary, poor, nasty, brutish, and short." (Thomas Hobbes)

There is, they declare, no purpose to the universe either. There is no meaning possible, since there is no meaning at all. Everything is purposeless and random.

Perhaps you have experienced purposelessness enough to smother your weariness with mere existing. The dreariness of your daily routine seems to illustrate an ugly conclusion about the obscenity of living. You try to make sense of life so you can justify your existence, but no meaningful purpose emerges. The tedium you face makes life vulgar. Activity accents monotony, living has turned gloomy and funereal. You know and experience the unintentional life.

Margaux Hemingway, tall, blond, and glamorous, achieved nearly instant renown in the 1970s as a supermodel. A New York fashion artist said in 1975 that she had "the face of a generation," representative and recognizable as "the most beautiful face in the Western hemisphere." Later that year she signed "the largest single advertising contract ever involving a female personality." The granddaughter of writer Ernest Hemingway, she changed her name from Margot to Margaux when she learned that her parents drank *Château Margaux* on the night of her conception. At the end of Margaux Hemingway's unhappy life she began to read her grandfather's books. Mr. Hemingway, the literary great, committed suicide. And so did she. Margaux had much decent activity going—she had just recently finished narrating a series on animals—but apparently enjoyed no purpose for living.[2] Activity in itself doesn't make for valid purpose.

THE PRICE OF PURPOSELESSNESS

If life contains no purpose, what can possibly make living worthwhile? Let me point out the cost of living without purpose.

No Purpose, No Worth

Greek mythology profoundly illustrates the *no-purpose, no-worth* connection in the story of Sisyphus. He was condemned to roll a stone up a mountain, let it roll down, roll it up again, let it roll down, and roll it up again—for life. If you are not captivated or energized by a purpose, you feel valueless. Every dawn finds you and your giant rock at the bottom of the hill again. Condemnation to mere existence is a heavy burden for suicide-optioned mortals.

Bruno Bettelheim took his life at age eighty-six on March 12, 1990. An expert on child psychology, a disciple of Freud, he was the director of the Orthogenic School for autistic and emotionally troubled children. His biographer notes that this brilliant subject "held, generally, that because life had no real purpose it was made livable only by pretending through fictions that it did."[3]

If life is not galvanized by valid purpose, there is no worth to it. I hope you are not caught in the iron web of purposelessness. Life might as well end. But, please, though you have the ability to end your life, don't take that option yet.

No Purpose, No Morals

If life is not undergirded by the right purpose, a sense of moral obligation will not influence nor order your smoke-and-mirror existence. Without purpose, morality becomes subjective and arbitrary. The Self referees good and evil, right and wrong. Anything will be permitted as long as it doesn't adversely affect one's Self. All moral decisions will be made by Me. All moral reality will be interpreted by Me. Nothing is right or wrong independent of Me.

This view leads to every person becoming right in his or her own eyes and ways. You would be right about everything. I could be right about everything, too. When we collide in our views, might becomes right. If all are equally right, only the powerful win by enforcing their "rightness" on the rest of us.

No Purpose, No Satisfaction

If life possesses no purpose, it will not satisfy. A friend of mine, in great desolation and needing immediate consolation in self-imposed isolation, was contemplating life—and taking his own! He decided he had nothing to live for, by, and on. That settled, he found himself dispensing epilepsy medicine to his pet dog when a disturbing thought hit him: "If I killed myself, who would give my dog its medication? In a few hours, the dog will go into distress, and eventually die." He told me later, "The need to give my dog medicine kept me alive." In those moments, both he and his dog hung between life and death by a slender thread.

My friend was right. The smallest of purposes can justify living. If life has no purpose, there is no good reason for life to possess value, elicit morality, or truly satisfy. Instead, it will be filled with anguish, instability, and aloneness. What kept him alive was a small purpose. An insignificant purpose is better than no purpose. As he admitted and I agreed, if he didn't have any purpose for which to live, then death did seem preferable.

I thought about my friend's dilemma. His dog never would have felt suicidal, even if its master died. Without the medication the pet would have lain down and died, but he wouldn't have lain down to die. We can excuse dogs for phlegmatic feelings, but they don't contemplate suicide because the brutes don't think about the purpose for their existence. Humans do. By the time we become self-aware, we discover that we are already playing the "game" called life. Yet some are tempted not to play at all. Death by suicide becomes more favorable than a purposeless life. Suicidal people feel it is better not to live and possibly win, than to live and definitely lose.

But suicide is not a moral option for you and me. While you may think it is better not to live and win than to live and lose, acting on that thought is worse than what you are simply considering. You are really saying that *it is better not to live and not know you lose, than to live and know you lose.* For you have no guarantee that you would win by dying. I know you may feel like caressing the notion of suicide. I know it may be far more compatible with your philosophy of life—the purposeless life. I salute you in wanting to live consistently. But don't snuff your life out yet. Briefly consider the implications of having a small, or low, purpose in life.

SMALL PURPOSE

Most people will theoretically espouse the belief that life carries purpose and that purpose sustains life, though that purpose may be minuscule. They quite readily acknowledge the existential inferences from the previous no-purpose position. Once you start reading a series of books like these on purpose, at least make it your purpose to finish it! Let's look at several ways we can pursue life.

Small Purpose, Soft Pursuit

A *small-purpose, soft-pursuit* way of living existentially vanquishes the *no-purpose, no-pursuit* view of life. Low purposes at least keep you from dying. Like my friend who stayed alive to dole out medicine to his puppy, many people identify arbitrary, casual, trivial purposes to find reasons not to die. But these are not going to furnish reasons for living. Simply staying alive is not quite living, but being alive provides enough justification to be indiscriminate and undiscerning—vaguely alive. Ponder this diverse sampling of small and low purposes that I have gathered from watching and talking to co-passengers in life over many miles and years:

- To count the rpm's of the ceiling fan
- To listen to music—especially Chopin, Mozart, and Dvorak
- To display clothes and jewelry
- To eat a meal
- To have sex
- To make love
- To get high
- To watch TV
- To travel—near or far
- To write a book
- To gain a degree
- To earn a living
- To start a business
- To keep the business
- To accumulate wealth
- To buy a house—a better, larger house
- To go on vacations
- To get a promotion
- To sell the business
- To play golf

It takes so little to keep humans from dying. Humans exhibit the unusual facility of converting minutiae into justifiable purposes for existence. Eventually, however, reality overtakes illusion and exposes delusion. How long can one keep living for these low purposes? Fan blades blur, music choices change, as do clothing styles, imbecilic TV makes ready-made food look good, and so on. Even moneymaking gets old. Perhaps, golf would keep us from death.

Small Purpose, Heavy Pursuit

To the company of the committed, playing golf furnishes no small purpose for life. I play *flog* (backward golf) better. They named the sport golf because all the other four-letter words were taken. The pros have to practice hard at duplicating my shots; I myself can never repeat them. For some of you, though you deny it, golf has become the ultimate purpose of your life. For others, fishing parallels the role of religion. Golf is better than fishing because you don't have to show anything to prove you did or didn't do something, though an eraser on your scoring pencil beckons its frequent use.

When it comes to purpose, as one writer puts it, "Even golfers are often at a loss to explain why they spend days walking over grassy hills trying to knock a small white ball into a cup."[4] That's intense pursuit of a small purpose.

In the mid-1980s, Nezar Hindawi's intense pursuit focused on blowing up an El Al airplane. He moved to England, met an Irish young lady, Anna Marie Murphy. She couldn't get a lifelong commitment out of him. Pregnant with his child, she was surprised one day when he asked her to marry him. He stipulated only one condition. He wanted the wedding to take place in the Holy Land. She was delighted. He made reservations for her travel on El Al, the highly secure Israeli airline. He helped pack her bags, and dropped her off at London's Heathrow to fly to Israel. He promised to meet her there for their wedding in a few days.

As Anna Marie Murphy submitted to rigorous check-in procedures, her suitcase set off a security alert. On opening it, officials found a bomb wired to blow up her jumbo plane after take off. I recall his day in court as Anna Marie looked at Nezar and asked, "How could you do this to me? How could you do this to your own baby?" We were stunned. As a result, airport security now routinely asks a seemingly stupid but standard question: "Did you pack your bags yourself?" Everyone would agree that blowing up a plane with four hundred people at thirty-five thousand feet revealed an intense pursuit of a small, but evil, purpose.

I don't doubt the *vitality* of your heavy pursuit of low purposes. I do question the *validity* of those small purposes in consuming your very life. I applaud your pursuit but am saddened by your sacrificial commitment, the waste of your brief life on the trivial made crucial, the minor made major, the marginal made essential.

Small purposes are whimsical.

They are whimsical because we have to invent them. Note the spirit of inventiveness in the following concoctions:

> ➤ We invent purpose out of relationships that promise intimacy.

> ➤ We invent purpose out of activities that provide resources to live.

> ➤ We invent purpose out of hobbies that relax us.

> ➤ We invent purpose out of our own selves to justify our existence.

Apparently, we humans can create purpose out of just about anything! I can begin a crusade to remove prefixes from German, or turn all green lights into stoplights, or pontificate on the blessing of burping every hour on the hour at two decibels in low alto. I could even start a Reburpican party or even a religion on that last cause. The fact that I hotly pursue a small purpose doesn't endow a bit of significance or value to that purpose.

Small purposes are relative.

We could debate the relative weight of a variety of small purposes. Your heavy pursuit of a small purpose may not be as obvious as religious golf or terrorism, but it is just as relative. One man's purpose is to make six million dollars; another's is to build a six-million-dollar house; and yet another's is to acquire a painting worth six million dollars. What you call small purpose may be my big purpose. But what if my "big" purpose is really a worthless purpose? How do I know if I am only chasing air bubbles?

Small purposes disappoint.

Interesting as they may be, low purposes eventually let you down. Once the challenge is conquered, disappointment sets in. A mother asks her five year old why he's sobbing uncontrollably. Between his wails he replies, "I've just learned how to tie my shoelaces." She congratulates her kid. "Marvelous," she heaps praise on him. "Not many five year olds can tie their shoes. You've done something no other kid in kindergarten can do. You can now teach others to do it. Terrific. You're becoming a young man. But why are you crying, son?"

"Because," he says, "now I'll have to do it every day for the rest of my life." Small purposes are like learning to tie shoelaces. Once you discover how to do them and have done them, they diminish in returning satisfaction. You were temporarily stimulated but not satisfied.

The advantage of small purposes is that they keep us from death—at least premature, self-inflicted fatality. Even the process and challenge of creating low purposes keep us from dying. Small purposes enable us to agree that we need some purpose to life, however arbitrary it may be. We need to be *about* some purpose for the sake of human worth, value, direction, satisfaction, and for a score of incidental benefits as well. *About-ness* distinguishes humanness from mere animal-ness. While an animal (and human) can unintentionally live without a purpose, a person (but not an animal) cannot unintentionally live *with* a purpose. Most hearts manufacture purposes to hold death at bay. This is why anything that is even remotely transferable as a plausible purpose for life gives us the will not to die. At the end, however, we will die.[5] Meanwhile, we must not throw life away.

STRONG PURPOSE

If a *no-purpose* life leads us to death, and a *small-purpose* life may keep us from death, a *strong-purpose* life energizes our existence. Beginning immediately. Small-purpose living caters only to *about-ness (busy-ness about any purpose)*. Strong-purpose living supplies *about-ness* and *beyond-ness (busy-ness with a justifiable purpose)*. For example, strong-purpose living could relate closely to

> raising children,
>
> serving people, or
>
> volunteering resources to meet human needs,

all of which exemplify justifiable pursuits.

Feeding the hungry, housing the homeless, lifting the downtrodden, liberating the oppressed, and strengthening the weak display strong purposes in life. The psychiatrist of Meaning, Viktor Frankl, observed the strong-purpose approach to personal life-sustenance even in the bleak harshness of concentration camps. Since Nazi guards did not discourage suicide attempts, "the goal was to try to prevent the act before the attempt. The healthy prisoners would remind the despondent that life expected something from them: a child waiting outside prison; work that remained to be completed." Preventing others' suicides was part of their strong purpose. It was "essential to keep practicing the art of living, even in a concentration camp."[6]

Justifiable strong purposes share a common thread in moving us beyond and away from what is transitory to what is truly valuable. For example, strong purposes shift the focus of our efforts from:

  things to people

  self-centeredness to other-centeredness

  appearances to realities

  ambivalence to accomplishment

  temporal to long-term results

  means to ends

  pragmatism to love, truth, duty, and beauty

  expediency to principle

  self-esteem to servanthood

  acquisition to impact

  existence to direction

  maintenance to legacy

  tentativeness to tenacity

  immediacy to ultimacy

In other words:

- ➤ Strong purposes are worth living for.

- ➤ Strong purposes keep you awake in the night for the right reasons.

- ➤ Strong purposes are worth dying for. And nobody is going to ask you to die for something you are not living for.

- ➤ Strong purposes are worth living for. Intentionally. Meaningfully. Freely. Enjoyably. Spontaneously. Joyfully. Indeed, purposefully!

BENEFITS OF STRONG PURPOSE

Just as small-purpose living eventually leads one to boredom, boredom returns the favor, confirming small-purpose living. Yet disappointment with small-purpose living could cause one to move on to a stronger purpose in life. The move beyond and away from small to strong purposes brings several advantages. Let me list three:

- ➤ *Inspiration and motivation.* Some philosophers feel that the problem of boredom, rather than finding purpose, is the prime challenge of human existence. If that is so, a strong purpose furnishes the real possibility of boredom prevention. Strong purposes wrap themselves around goals, work, and tasks, and motivate accomplishment. Strong purposes inspire and move us forward; they unleash creative juices and justify activity.[7]

- ➤ *Satisfaction and actualization.* Some psychologists place fulfillment and significance on the top rung of the hierarchy of human needs. Strong purposes provide the means to achieve great satisfaction in life.

➤ *Destination and direction.* Some preachers exult in ultimate destination, endowing justification for present existence, appropriate decision-making, adequate exertion, and meaningful direction. It is better to expend energy intentionally going to some place than simply keeping an airplane aloft. Stronger purposes show us where we want to go and show the way.

A strong purpose life ranks as qualitatively better than a small purpose life and bears no resemblance to a no purpose life.

DANGERS IN STRONG PURPOSE

If we are aware and conscientious, the benefits of high purposes could outweigh their dangers. Yet dangers attend high purpose, or more rightly, inadequately justifiable high purposes.

Object-illusion. It is possible to pursue low purposes as though they were high purposes. I pointed out earlier that one's level of commitment doesn't affect the quality of purpose. One can be highly committed to a low purpose, even as I may be lightly committed to a high purpose. We endeavor to give substance to mirages by sleight of mind, the illusory tactic of turning invalid purposes into high purposes. Building an elaborate house versus building a happy family is a case in point. Constructing a stunning house is low purpose translated into high purpose if we assume a necessary connection between a grand house and a great home life. That connection is an illusion. High purposes must be substantiated as high, regardless of the intensity of personal commitment.

Motive-confusion. The delusion of chasing the wrong object is as bad as the confusion of wrong motives in striving after the right object. A couple has invested extraordinary energy and money into restoring the run-down house of an Episcopalian parsonage in Dallas. They struggle with confused motives. With self-confessed honesty they ask, "Are we restoring the building to serve the community or to pridefully display and be appreciated for our interior decorating talent and monetary generosity to the church?" When it comes to mixed motives, the distinction between low purpose and high purpose becomes slight and slim. High purposes are fragile, not in themselves, but in connection with wrong motives. We cross a thin line by the kind of motives we think generate the activity, confusing them with the actual motives which call us to pursue the high purpose. We think our motives are good but we are unable to distinguish these from our true motives.

Means-end fission. Making money is a neutral undertaking. Making money to feed one's family is good. Making money the wrong way to feed a family is evil, although feeding the family is laudable. When means are independent of the ends in our lives, we can deceive ourselves, rationalize our immorality, and legitimize anything under the guise of a high purpose. Here a high purpose demands an immoral means to attain it and thus becomes demonic. To echo a now unpopular dictum, "The end doesn't justify the means." International organizations undertake excellent work in some of the most miserable places of the world. However, some officials think they are entitled to an opulent lifestyle and financial waste because they are serving the oppressed. Peace among warring nations, a high purpose, doesn't demand monetary waste and mishandling of expense account privileges. We must distinguish between means and ends, but we shall not divide them.

Purpose-result fusion. While we don't divide means from

ends, we must keep purpose and result separate. Therein lies a critical distinction that will ease many areas of self-doubt, including the evaluation of your motives. A colleague received a high compliment after a lecture to corporate executives on "conflict resolution." Check the bracketed words added to this note he received:

> The real difference between your approach and all the management organizations we've dealt with in the past is the bottom line. You're interested in helping people first [purpose], and covering costs is secondary [result]. Secular organizations are interested in showing a profit [purpose], and if they help someone in the process [result], that's okay.

When you fuse purpose and results, wrong purpose often begins to dominate. Even if the right purpose draws you, a results-oriented measure of the validity of the purpose will disqualify the quality of the purposes. Some purposes are high purposes whatever the results. It is good for firefighters to expend all their energies to fight an apartment fire to save just one infant life—*especially* an infant life! Firefighters do not give greater effort to firefighting if there are more lives than less to save.

Your pursuit of a high purpose may not yield the kind of result(s) you desire. When quantifiability of results determines the qualifiability of purposes, you are susceptible to environmentally determined perceptions of success. Quality and quantity, purpose and result are tied together, but only in a peripheral way. Bigger results doesn't mean better purposes. Those who smuggle illicit and banned drugs justify their purposes by their results. Separate these aspects in your soul and you can persevere in doing right, doing good, and doing well—better.

Meaning-"in," purpose-"of" delusion. Similar to the object-illusion of turning low purposes to high purposes is the delusion of taking what provides meaning in life and viewing it as the purpose of life. Culture often dictates in what we are supposed to find life's meaning. We pursue high purposes that are not ours to pursue and turn them into the purpose of life. Yes, meanings in life call for your human best. You struggle against an evil and vanquish the disease. That gives meaning. You work hard to gain the best that money can buy. That asserts your identity. Your philanthropic efforts entitle you to have buildings named after you. That provides significance. Yet, seeking meanings in life will stifle the purpose-of-life question.

High purposes will give you meaning in life, but they do not reveal the purpose of life. The purpose of life will relate to the highest purpose that possibly exists. That purpose of life can be the foundation, the framework, for the multiple dimensions that yield meanings in life. However, meanings in life shouldn't be mistaken for the purpose of life. Without an overall strategy, to suppose that small conquests equal final victory is mental voodoo. Capturing pawns off your opponent while he is chasing your queen is not an even exchange. Going for pawns without an overall strategy is worse. I'm glad you've been lucky until now.

Good-good tension. The worst danger of many high purposes is not the legitimacy of the pursuits but the limitations of the pursuer.[8] We are limited as to our resources—time, energy, money. If there is no way to prioritize among the many goods we can pursue, we will be torn by immediate and subjective considerations.[9] What is emotionally closest to me gets the best of me. Family love is an illustration of the point. "After spending almost 200 nights away from home on missions in the last year, he said he can no longer sacrifice his family to the demands of the Air Force."[10] Like that pilot, nothing can compete with my family for my attention. No cause, however great and worthy it is, will receive the scantiest nod because one good competes with another good in life. Eventually, I realize I am the closest to me, the best for me! And even my family doesn't take precedence over my self-centeredness. The inexplicable madness of mothers killing their own children for the sake of gaining new lovers points to having no big purpose that helped the anguished person choose between two seemingly good options.

In addition to the moral ambiguity, you face the practical difficulty of not having enough time each day to deal with a multiplicity of good options. Busyness accents the confusion of a choice between the *goods*. Indecisiveness overtakes us in conflicting desires. Instability becomes our hallmark as the urgent overtakes the important in ongoing tension.

We also face the limitation of one lifetime. The specter of aging never leaves us. The possibility of sickness hangs around. As intimated earlier, death will get the best of us, all of us, even those who follow high purposes. Consequently, I don't want to live my life having to choose between equally good options without a way to choose between them. Do you?

SUPREME PURPOSE

Many worthwhile, solid purposes do compete and conflict with each other for our limited resources of time, energy, and money. To help us negotiate among many goods, or, better, to prioritize and sanctify all the goods, we need an overarching standard, an outside purpose, to serve as an ontological foundation for all of life—organizing its many dimensions, complexities, and opportunities. Small and strong purposes function in foundational ways, but a supreme purpose that underlies strong purposes addresses numerous additional *human* issues.[11] The basic marker of humanness, the reason we need purposes at all, is answered by that supreme purpose. A single, deepest purpose meets the core needs and wants of being human. We then have a genuine and abundant *human* life to live, personally and intentionally.

Let us look at some uniquely shared features of the supreme purpose for any and all human existence. Later, we will look at a number of the benefits resulting from supreme purpose.[12]

We need and want unity in the interior of our lives.

We feel stressed, if not lynched, by numerous commitments and options to pursue. Interior unity will bestow quiet, inner harmony. Morally good, personally beneficial, and socially useful opportunities present themselves for our immediate consideration and extended involvement. A supreme purpose provides the touchstone for wise decision making about equally good opportunities. The cohesion we seek in the multiplicity of demands, in the busyness of activities, and in the choice between fine options derives from the supreme and foundational purpose.

We need and want totality, a totality that justifies the multiple, sweeping regions of our lives.

A concrete and comprehensive purpose organizes life's fragments. It assumes the foundational role, subsumes the segments, and consumes our timetable and activities. Totality in the unity also provides for the creativity we need to develop the dimensionalities we experience in personal existence. Is there a supreme purpose that brings my personal life, family life, work life, and service under it, in totality and in unity?

We need and want objectivity to our lives.
This supreme purpose prevents us from falling into illusion, delusion, and confusion that result from a lack of wise foundation.[13] This deepest purpose must come from above and beyond the human situation. Existentialists have eloquently reminded us that we cannot find meaning or purpose *within* individual or corporate life. *Beyond*ness and *above*ness go together in objectifying the importance of the supreme, foundational purpose.[14]

We need and want universality to the supreme purpose.
A supreme purpose must apply to all people, and that equally. A beyond-human purpose possessing inclusive appeal. Yet, there must also be substance to that universality. It is easy to construct a universal purpose in abstraction as the religions have done—be good, or do good, or feel good. "Goodness" without definition is open to the least common denominator in faddish values or trendy majority interpretations and is therefore shallow or superficially universal. The supreme purpose claims all people in the *depths* of their concrete, personal existence.

We need and want purity in our pursuits of high purposes.
Søren Kierkegaard's book *Purity of Heart Is to Will One Thing*[15] is a most profound statement of spiritual existence. He states, "A pure heart is first and last a bound heart"—bound to the highest purpose. The highest purpose filters the impurities of motives and allows a more pure will to emerge. We must *will* only the highest purpose—as the passion, mission, and vision *of* life, as we *do* many other purposes—as passions, missions, and visions *in* life.

We need and want identity from an absolute, timeless source.
A part of our identity derives from personal meaning we gain from relative indices of success such as performance, possessions, and so on. Instead, pursuing the supreme purpose gives us a better orientation for identity, an umbrella to cover us during a self-flagellating downpour, a liberating protection from circumstantially or emotionally interpreted self-worth. The lack of an absolute source for self-identity may lead to an emphasis on gaining significance in the second half of a successful life. But we don't know when the second half starts nor ends. The pursuit of identity in significance can actually keep us from usefulness in the supreme purpose throughout life—including early life, whether successful or not.

We need and want clarity to our motives in self-examination and expression.
Is there an absolute, supreme purpose that is foundational in its own status? Is there something that I could pursue for its own sake, without shrewd calculation? We don't want to simply "perform" for a watching, adoring, gullible public, though the talented always do and will. However, the awareness of our unclear motives in light of the supreme purpose provides a good read on our imperfect motives. Further, we desire clarity in verbally stating and sharing the supreme purpose. Without clarity we will wallow in confusion and abstraction—again the problem of religion *per se*. I don't want any more self-made confusion. The supreme purpose needs to be simple and straightforward so I can understand it myself; so I can understand myself; so that I can recommend it to you.

We need and want a "supreme" **purpose** *of life supporting our other purposes in life.*

The supreme purpose is not simply a concept, it must become an influential, concrete reality in our lives. It is *applied* philosophy, theology, and spirituality. The supreme purpose will provide the foundational underpinning, the ground-level infrastructure, and a personal vision for our future in all of life's dimensions, responsibilities, activities, and opportunities.

The supreme purpose begins with the undergirding purpose of life comprising the foundational passion, the daily mission, and the overall vision for an intentional life. On that undergirding purpose we will begin to build; by it we will start to live; for its sake and our own sake, we will pursue the rest of today and all our tomorrows.

An Intentional Life

The state trooper grew increasingly curious as he observed some strange behavior—a trucker pulling over, getting out of his cab, beating his hand on both sides of his truck, climbing back in, and rejoining traffic. The driver repeated this odd sequence every few miles. After three times, the trooper's suspicions escalated to probable cause. He pulled the truck over and asked the driver to explain his actions. The trucker said, "It's simple. My load limit is two tons and there are four tons' worth of chickens back there. If I don't keep half of them airborne, I'm in trouble." The man was ticketed for the extra weight. There has been no news on how the chickens fared.

> *Chaos reigns within,*
> *Reflect, repent and reboot,*
> *Order shall return!*
>
> **⟐A COMPUTER ERROR**
> **HAIKU POEM**

Does that trucker remind you of someone you know rather well? You realize your life should not carry the load you've placed on it. You practice ingenuity to keep juggling the weight while breaking personal limitations to transport life wherever you think you should take it. While people watch your behavior askance, they are not going to ticket you. We are glad that you stop often enough to keep some of life's weight airborne. But the trooper will find you someday right in the middle of your obsessions, juggling acts, and creative maneuverings. Meanwhile, the extra weight and internal chaos may kill you before you repent, reflect, and reload your life.

The trucker mistook activity for purpose, motion for mission, being legal for effectiveness, chaos for normal. By contrast, let me here set the tone for the intentional life, so you can be purposeful about the deepest, most valid, vital dimension(s) of life. I will define and outline an intentional life. Most importantly, you will see how purpose plays out in the intentional life.

NOT!
NOT A LIFE RULED BY OBSESSIONS

The intentional life cannot be ruled by obsessions. Obsessions are unsuitable candidates for ultimacy. Obsessions distract. Instead of being occupied with life in its totality, obsessions get you preoccupied with some aspect of life as though it were all of life.

> The astounding corporate energy put into the mundane-ness of daily removal of facial hair helps illustrate preoccupation-turned-obsession. At the Gillette shaving razor factory, two hundred men and thirty women—all Gillette employees—pass through the test lab. Another 2,700 off-site shavers test products at home. In the in-house lab, "researchers can count the razor strokes, clock the length of de-whiskerization and observe split-face shaving, in which dueling products are tested on opposite sides of a subject's face. Shavers then peck at computer score pads to rate such facts as

comfort, nicks and cuts, and the spreadability of shaving gel. If it sounds a little *obsessive* (the author's word), try visiting Gillette's British research center, "where they have determined 'that the average man spends 140 days of his life removing 27 feet of facial hair, and that a whisker is 70 percent easier to cut after being soaked two minutes in warm water.' . . . "The quest for the perfect shave has *preoccupied* mankind for eons."[1]

Check the two italicized words in the quotation above. Connect them for sage advice. Whatever *preoccupies* you is your *obsession*.

Is it work?

Is it family?

Is it sports?

Is it nature?

Is it hobbies?

Is it sex?

Is it profit?

Is it "more"?

Whatever preoccupies you reveals your obsession. Short-term "obsessions" serve well for immediate productivity and efficiency. Productive energy given to obsessive behavior supplies its own rationalization. However, uncontrolled obsessions lead to burnout, anger, depression, conflicts with loved ones, ethical compromises, relational risks, and eventual despair. You've got to decide whether your obsessions are worth the cost and energy put into them. It simply won't profit you to gain the whole world and lose your soul.

Obsessions carry spiritual power.

Fixation on an unworthy object causes a certain spiritual commitment—a deep-sea dive into obsessions. You get engrossed in work, family, sports, and so on—completely immersed in ocean depths when the oxygen tank runs out. Fighting for life, you call for help. But your awareness comes too late. Your obsession, while superstitiously monopolizing your attention now, has also drowned you. It has extinguished the fire in the bottom of your bosom.

Now obsessions provide strategic spiritual power for businesses and sustain organizations, even civilizations. Consumer-based economies rely on obsessive, and possibly impulsive, responses of their participants. Obsessions about temporal objects, however, are not good for individuals. Businesses, organizations, and empires eventually cease to exist (e.g., the Roman civilization or the East India Shipping Company), but individuals will never cease to exist. Only a preoccupation with God, who created us as *eternal* persons, rises to the level of a worthy personal obsession. Any other entrant is *non grata* and leads to a godless eternal experience. By definition, only One merits our complete and undivided attention. Yet the startling truth behind our passionate preoccupation with God is that it enhances our love and enjoyment of all other worthy objects. Indeed, that passion for God prevents the obsession from becoming unhealthy by God's own insistence that we love Him by also loving neighbors, fellow eternal beings.

Obsessions don't allow you to make a life.

Obsessions encourage you to make a killing. Do you know what you are killing? Simple pleasures are reckoned "wasteful." You don't consider a coffee break, a vacation trip, friends dropping in unannounced, or regular playing with your kids as good uses of time, though they are good uses of life. Unless lower-case obsessions yield to a grand passion, a large mission, and a powerful vision, you will practice daily self-destruction of life and time. You need a supreme purpose to keep life obsession-free. Obsessions provide erroneous foundations and mistaken absolutes.

Obsessions signal warnings.

You can tell you are ruled by obsessions in life whether related to self, family, work, or service. Here are some danger signs.

Obsessions lurk if and when you turn the dimensions of life—personal, family, work, and service or any part of them—into objects of unquestioned devotion.

You pursue out-of-place priorities when dimensions of life become your passion. When you turn any dimension of life or any part of a dimension of life into the passion of life, you fall into idolatry. You are worshiping creation rather than the Creator. Having become idolatrous, you find it hard to hear Jesus' words to His disciples, "If anyone comes to Me and does not hate his own father and mother and wife and children and brothers and sisters, yes, even his own life, he cannot be My disciple" (Luke 14:26, NASB). These intense relationships make up the dimensions of life where purpose interrupts and passion intervenes. Important as they may be, they cannot turn into obsessions. These dimensions form the framework of a disciple's purpose. Indeed, the right object of passion must intrude and control these areas of life.

In school, studies and grades change to obsessions. In recreation, tennis, travel, or television cause fixations. Even your spouse, whom you should unconditionally love absolutely, could translate into an obsession. A well-to-do couple with two small children and two new European automobiles told me they "hope to begin giving to the Lord's work after we lay and pay for the carpet in our new house." A house is a critical sub-dimension of personal and family life. In this case a good dimension shifted into a transgressive, ingressive obsession. How do we live under obsessions? How do we live with dimensions?

What weighs on you as your present obsession? Work? Where lies your exclusive loyalty? Family? What have you set your heart upon? Your public persona? What seizes your being? Earning more? You need a purpose and passion check—an inner audit.

We all need a purpose to live for. But if we are passionate about an erroneous purpose, it turns out to be an obsession. There is only one appropriate obsession. Only passion for One, after the One purpose, is correct and healthy, necessary and sufficient, for a life well lived, for time well used. Thus, loving God and living for Him in life's various dimensions could never turn into an inappropriate obsession. You will never go wrong wanting Him above anyone or anything else.

Obsessions prowl if and when you don't invite the intervention of God into life's realities.

Again, ruled by wrongful obsessions, you live a flawed and independent life. Without God in charge, classic, obsessional behavior manifests itself in your claiming omniscience and playing omnipotent in specific situations. "Rather than face an awareness of the impossibility of being omniscient and acknowledging his human limitations, the obsessional concludes that if only he knew more and tried harder, he could achieve these goals."[2] When you do not invite God into your life, you play God in your life. Instead, soliciting the influence of God in your life keeps you from obsessions and again, therefore, from idolatry.

It happens to me, too. Let's say I face a problem between two of my peers at work. My experience, knowledge, and giftedness as a leader come into play as I attempt to solve the difficulty in an equitable way. Both sides of the argument contain merit. I don't want to be unfair. If my confusion remains, I go to consultants who give of their accumulated wisdom in these situations (for a fee, of course!). Their principles generally apply but don't address specific concerns. I am still at a loss. I hit business magazines, intuitive gauges, and yellowing notes on leadership. I get caught in indecision because of a relational problem between people I like and respect. I feel the need for total awareness of all the facts in the given situation to perfectly solve the problem. In all of this, I have not invited the perspective of the Father in heaven, who gives wisdom for all who lack it, admit the lack, and ask for it (James 1:5). It is at this point I suspect my daily responsibilities overtake my enthusiasm for God. Only when I begin easing the process by instantly, firstly, and regularly asking God for wisdom by going to His Word for counsel, by trusting in His leadership of every situation, do I become free from obsessional living.

Prayerlessness is a candid mark of slavery to obsessions. If you take all the problems of all your dimensions to God, then God still is God over all the dimensions of your life. The longer I wait to "bother" Him, the more I will be bothered by objectives, thrusts, and even my mission shifting to wrongful obsession and idolatrous passion. I pray not to be obsessed wrongly and not to pursue the wrong obsession. Failure to first consult God in prayer reveals a commitment to myself as the solution to life. Faith in myself is not denying my Self. The Self interferes as I seek to love, glorify, and serve God as the only worthy candidate for total life purpose.

Obsessions stalk if and when you pursue the urgent and the immediate of life's dimensions, with no large purpose in mind.

Wrongful preoccupations make you easy prey for obsessions. While the Internet was still young, a heterosexual young man, relatively happily married, on a whim one day posed as a woman on-line. He pulled it off beautifully. People soon began to respond to him, more precisely, to his false identity and alter ego that he had set up. Within a short amount of time, he discovered he was unable to undo this creation of his. He approached schizophrenia. He was two persons, not one. It got more interesting from there, with no purpose by which to live or compass by which to travel in cyberspace.

He fell in love with a woman on-line. Since he himself was posing as a woman, it was a lesbian relationship. A heterosexual man posing as a woman, falling in love with another woman, in an on-line lesbian affair. A curiosity turned into an obsession. Each night he excused himself from the family dinner table, went upstairs, and put in four or five hours on the Net. He ended up getting a divorce. Obsession got the better of him, for he admitted it wouldn't be possible for him to reveal the truth of his gender to his lover. "I expect to go on the Net for the rest of my natural life as a woman. I can't shut off this person I have created. I can't turn her off. One of us will not log on one day, and then we'll be gone."[3]

Earlier I touched on translating family love into an obsession. The urgencies that need immediate attention because of the pressures of life, the dependencies of children, and the exigencies of running a home are numerous and varied. Fortunately, your family is made up of people (even though we all wonder about that when the kids are teenagers), and people are certainly more worthy than things for your loving attention. Yet we need an alert. The heavy emphasis on "family first" as a means to prevent family breakdown must include a caution. If your family is first in your life, you'll become imbalanced. How much time should you give your family when work demands large chunks of time? Which one in your family needs the most attention? Should you attend to your husband whose love you are losing or to the infant at your breast whose life must be sustained?

Sociological studies buttress the anecdotal evidence: in order to preserve emotional health and provide family cohesion, putting family first in one's life is better than neglecting the family. But observers find children of such "family-first-families" grow into selfish, inward-looking, and purposeless adults. Suddenly, no one pays them the attention their parents did. As children they needed to be unleashed into a greater purpose for existence than mere personal and family happiness. The kids missed out on lessons about the need to sacrifice for greater causes. They didn't know much about service or self-denial. A family-first campaign affirms families, especially guilt-ridden, neglectful dads, who need to be motivated to pay attention. Yet that focus also communicates to depraved kids (that's all of us) that they never need to grow up into responsible, outward-looking, serving adults.

Your family life needs to fit into a larger purpose, a purpose that is comprehensive, constructive, and cohesive. That purpose can't leave out the family nor destroy it. But your children should never be confused about who is most important in your life. And that is neither yourself nor them.

I remember heading to an economically broken West African country. Our children were twelve, ten, and eight years old at that time. As a family we had discussed the terrible deprivation in the sub-Saharan region—one doctor for thousands of people; only two hundred hospital beds for the whole nation; average male life expectancy at thirty years; children needing basics of food and clothing.

Two days before I embark on an overseas trip, our family usually experiences a severe case of separation anxiety. I begin to wonder why I accepted the invitation. My wife, Bonnie, wishes I wasn't going. The children wonder why their dad is leaving again, so soon, for so long. I was leaving on December 31 that year, and would have to miss our Watchnight service tradition. Fifteen minutes before I left for the airport our eight year old showed up with hands behind her back. I knew she had a surprise for me. Thinking it was a farewell note of love, I asked, "What do you have there, sweetheart?"

She brought her hands to the front, filled with the proceeds from her emptied piggy bank. She replied: "Daddy, we've been talking about the poor children where you are going. I want you to give this to them." My wife and I teared up at her sensitivity. Then I shouted to her older brothers, "Hey, your sister has given all her money for the children in West Africa. What are you guys going to do about it?" They leaped off their seats, emptied their coffers, and brought monies as well. My heart rejoiced and trembled not only because my kids gave their all but especially because this trip was not mine alone. My family owned the ministry vision, the service part of my intentional life.

I attempt to plug our family, as beloved as they are in my life, into a larger purpose for our existence. To that end, our family has traveled on several overseas service trips, where Bonnie and the kids often teach Bible classes and lead in singing. In Fiji, they ministered to 150 different children in ten classes over a week. At this writing, the Lord has orchestrated a weekly "Boy's Bible Bash with Mr. Richard" in our home. Last night, our second son and I wrote a theme for the next bash.

I am grateful. I would give my life for my wife and kids. But they are not my obsessions. They are part of a larger purpose, the supreme purpose for my life, our lives.

NOT A LIFE RULED BY NERVES

A life ruled by purpose avoids the rule of nerve endings. The intentional life does not function at the whim of tendencies and inclinations and calls it life. Living on the edge of one's nerves facilitates survival more than arrival, as you cater to urgencies and emergencies. Muddling from day to day without a larger purpose victimizes you. Circumstances overwhelm you. You can't live with steady superiority over the immediate stresses that seek to rule you. A nerve-racking life, thriving on chaos, cannot be sustained in the long run. Nerve-racking results in life-wrecking.

The human experiment with absolute freedom starts in adolescence. Biologically and behaviorally, nerve-ending living leads to addictions in the name of freedom. Finding a spiritual home on our own, in our seemingly bleak universe, runs into major obstacles. We would like this spiritual home to be eternal and stable but find our activities bound by time and change. Like homing pigeons who lose their way due to cellular interference or climatic changes, we follow new impulses. We turn with hope to dopey solutions, literally to heroin or cocaine, or metaphorically to any stimulant. We finally get addicted to a new slavery in the name of freedom. We even barter away human, appreciable freedom in the pursuit of unlimited freedom normally reserved by religions for their gods. Fix after fix, be it erotica, smoking, or shopping, we can't live without temporary fixes.

But there is no freedom without accompanying consequences. The consequence should be one's purpose. Without purpose you are left with isolation, anxiety, and despair. Nerve-ending living leads to arbitrariness as you run from your primary purpose for existence to self-gratifying or ego-pleasing fixes in work, fun, or addictions. Nerve-ending living blinds you from contemplating destiny and purpose.

In terms of sensuality, nerve-ending living reduces you to instinctual living. Your daily decisions express body-based appetites. You live to please them. You are bound to and abound in abnormality. Neuroscience increasingly confirms how any kind of "addiction appears to steal the brain's normal ability to sense pleasure."[4] Eventually, the drugs taken can't even produce a high but must be ingested just to feel right. Nerve-ending living is abnormality turned normal once addiction overpowers your purpose for existence and becomes its reason.

Nerve-ending living does possess a fun twist. If nerve-racking living merely survives on chaos, nerve-ending living positively thrives on pleasure. Flittering from one option to another, from shop to shop, partner to partner, led by your nerves, reveals no strategy or purpose for life. Nerve-ending living shows only passing interest in urgencies and emergencies. But it lives on erections and orgasms, physically and emotionally. Sex guru Nancy Friday wrote 589 pages on the assumption that learning to love one's genitals is the way to solve the world's problems![5] No wonder then that the world's most recognizable symbol, more so than the golden arches of a fast-food restaurant and the stylized italics of soft drinks, is the condom. Living to appease nerve endings threatens to wipe out half the African continent and a tenth of humanity.

Nerve-ending living lives by nerve-arousing emotions. The Dallas Cowboys evoke delirium in our city, especially when they play in the Super Bowl. Ryan, my oldest son, is particularly committed to them—a dimension becoming an obsession. My travel schedule allows me to watch only one of three or four games they play each season. One year, the Cowboys' appearance in the Super Bowl conflicted with my travel schedule. I would have liked to watch that game on television with family and friends. Unfortunately, I was to speak that same day in southern India to a significant audience with tremendous needs, the last stop of a longer trip. Even gaining twelve hours couldn't bring me back to the U.S. in time for the opening kickoff. If I canceled that engagement, I would arrive home at 4:30 P.M. for the 5:00 P.M. start.

My emotions churned in turmoil as priorities conflicted over the decision. What should I do? Come back home? Minister there? I went back to my purpose. Is my family my purpose of life? If it were, there was no question where I should be that Sunday evening—in front of the television adulating over the best football game of the year—along with my son. My life purpose, however, does not include watching all possible championship games with my children. Don't get me wrong. I immensely enjoy watching football with my kids, and I especially enjoy watching them watching football. I have often taken earlier flights in order to spend weekends with my family. But my purpose is larger and deeper than what I would simply love to do at any given time. So I gently and humbly explained to Ryan how much I wanted to watch the big game with him. Yet I had to choose between speaking to two thousand spiritually needy people and being with him at the Super Bowl party. I asked, "Would you mind taping the game and we could watch it on Monday night together?" He swiftly replied, "Sure! As long as I get to watch the game while it is going on!"

My conflicting values, emotions, and conscience were eased. Ryan learned that life's decisions were to follow life's purpose. I began the overseas trip. In Frankfurt, Germany, I received news that my ailing father-in-law had passed away, and I had to return home after all. We watched the game together live, without having compromised my purpose. Had I to miss many special events with my children, I would have to reevaluate my commitments at this season of life with young children. Often, purpose will conflict with inclinations. You must pursue a worthy purpose in order to make the right decisions when faced with an internal conflict of values. Or you will be left to your whim at each turn of life. You will be left to choosing whatever you feel like doing at a given moment. You will be ripped and shredded on the inside.

Nerve-ending living is reactive rather than intentional. Reactive living helps in short-term activities—for example, should we eat out tonight, and where should we eat out? Circumstances will surround you, and you must react to them in real time. You must make decisions based on your present perception of the issues. Yet, I don't recommend reactive living as a strategy for long-term or sustained effectiveness.

Recently a friend groaned over his twenty-one-year-old son. This dad called his son a "jerk from the time he was two." Since I wanted to learn from his foibles, I asked if he would have done anything differently. "Yes," he replied. "I would have spent more time doing jerky things with him even though I didn't like them. However, growing my business was my passion. Too many business problems took me away from my family." The last nineteen years have been firefighting years, fighting his son's belligerence, his business fluctuations, his wife's moods, and his life's turns. No human being can effectively control a simmering nineteen-year-old cauldron hurriedly. His reactive living, dictated by the immediate circumstances of business life, avoided creative commitment to family priority, and evaded any long-term commitment to the ultimately important.

Again, much of life is reactive, or better, responsive, because of our inability to predict the future. We must learn to be firefighters. Firemen react to or respond to fires. But they have already aligned the practices and procedures of firefighting to the purposes and principles of their job. They react, but they react well, because the purpose of firefighting has already been defined. The right purpose, similarly, allows you to cope with differing, competing, and threatening demands of present dimensions, with the spiritual resources of an ultimate purpose and a unique vision for your life.

NOT A LIFE RULED BY COINCIDENCES

The primary sources for discovering one's life purpose in current spirituality are "synchronicity" and "intuition." Built on the worldview of New Age spirituality and depth psychology, these approaches view human beings as spiritually positive realities, born with purpose, already living in mystery beyond simple cause and effect. We must "face life like detectives—gleaning the meanings, the silver linings, the windows of opportunity, that lie hidden in what occurs around us."[6] Synchronicity is "an apparently chance encounter that nevertheless seems cosmically orchestrated. If we are to align ourselves to our purpose, it will be necessary to recognize and open ourselves to these catalyzing events."[7] These coincidences appeal to our inner needs.

So, spiritually sensitive people today look to "synchronic" events, getting in touch with their intuitions, "to move into the right spot for synchronicity to unfold and lead us forward."[8] Since these people are looking intently for coincidences, many sources for direction emerge—television, movies, horoscopes, Q Balls,[9] fortune cookies—whatever.[10] Even taxicab drivers who listen sympathetically and offer helpful advice turn out to be helpful guides for life.[11] These gurus find meaning in "any kind of odd coincidence," by posing questions like "what does this coincidence seem to suggest? Does it seem to be a yes or no answer to any question I have been subtly asking? Do I feel energized? Does this feel like a go-ahead signal? Do I feel a draw to see this person again?"[12]

I do understand the desire to make meaning out of life, to read direction from experiences, and to receive guidance from any kind of coincidence. We all seek discovery moments, defining events, and decisive incidents—except that our *interpretation* of experience and *integration* of coincidence into direction depends on worldview premises. Coincidences are providences only in a theistic worldview where a personal God gives personal attention to His children.

Without a vibrant, personal relationship with the God of the "coincidence," you can explain away any incident as an accident. You then remain emotionally paralyzed without a definite interpretation of the incident, stranded in the private meaning that you try to impose on an experience that can be interpreted in many indefinite ways. But *you* are the one looking for meaning in the first place. How can the blind or the lost find himself? If he is not blind or lost, he doesn't need to find himself. But if he is blind and lost, he needs external help for sight and position. How can you trust your interpretation of an event when you are looking for *any* event to communicate much meaning to you? A solution is only possible if you belong to the God of all events and relate rightly to Him in the first place. God, your creator, sustainer, and judge, is sheer light and understanding. "He knows what lies in darkness, and light dwells with him," declares Daniel the Hebrew prophet (2:22). You want this God to help you discern among incidents that resemble coincidences, and then interpret and integrate them in a life lived under God's personal providence and superintendence.

Let's say you wonder if you should change jobs. You wake up tomorrow morning with a flat tire. What are you supposed to make of that coincidence? Are you not to go to work? Or are you to go late? Or are you to take public transportation and learn the bus routes? Or are you to get a job where you can walk to work? Do you change jobs or change the tire? and on and on. A hundred interpretations are possible for any incident, event, or experience. Your interpretation will take distinctive turns if you interpret it by yourself or seek God's meaning in it. You are left to making sense of the dark when you are blind.

Since coincidental life resembles a dark attic, you manifest two natural problems: you are blind, and you are in the dark. If you can see but live in the dark, all you need is some light. You can't interpret in the dark, unless a light shines through. But if you are blind, it doesn't matter if light exists. A blind translator assisted me each night I spoke in Gangtok, Sikkim, a remote Himalayan location in the northeast corner of India. Electrical power to the community hall frequently failed. We speakers could hear the people's disappointment as light disappeared. My blind translator knew what happened each time the audience groaned. He asked them to excuse him if he made any translation mistakes now that the lights were off! They roared, for it didn't make any difference to him if the lights were on or off. Even though we were in the dark, as long as he interpreted my comments, they could understand what I was saying. Unless you are spiritually awakened, you can't interpret your coincidences or circumstances. Yet even those who can see need an interpreting light in the middle of the darkness. As long as you attempt to intuitively read synchronicity, you will remain imprisoned in that dark attic without a flashlight. But don't worry! It wouldn't have made any difference to have to interpret if, in the first place, you couldn't see anything at all that needed interpretation. The only advantage a blind person has in the dark is that it doesn't make a difference to him if the light is on or off.

So interpreting coincidence rightly would only be possible under two conditions. You need to be able to see *and* possess light in the darkness. Spiritual advisors want you to be able to light your way when you can't see in the first place. All they can promise is a better experience of the darkness. Once you can see, though, you can learn to personally interpret life's important experiences. Then coincidences can be evaluated rightly, given appropriate weight, and prioritized correctly for personal guidance. To blind and lost people, intuitions about coincidence are neither synchronic nor useful. They are unsuitable and scary, leaving you at the mercy of personal impulse, capricious interpretation, and a harmful combination in finding life purpose.

Neither obsessions, nor nerves, nor coincidences help us to pursue life's purpose. Being compulsive about impulsiveness and impulsive about compulsiveness leads to spiritual and psychological disaster. A dwarfing of the soul follows and should not surprise us. When we are addicted to obsessions, whims, or self-interpreted accidents, we elevate something less than ultimate to near divine terms in our lives. We turn relatives to absolutes, the contingent to foundational, the conditional to unconditional, the provisional to supremacy, the finite to the infinite, the particular to general. A sense of "wasted-ness" fills your soul, and you wonder whether you muddled your life away—ruled by the urgent operation of the nerves; meddled your life away—ruled by obsessions; or messed up your life—ruled by limited understandings of coincidences.

We need a supreme purpose that is universal, absolute, and foundational. We need an unconditional, worthy, infinite purpose to live for, a passion to live by, which turns into a platform to live on and arranges parameters to live within.

MORE THAN!

We have seen what the intentional life is *not*. Let's look at what the purposeful life is *more than*. Personal purpose is more specific than general purpose when we are building a life. We may be right or wrong at the ground floor level. Even if we are right on the ground floor, we must be careful about what the upper levels denote. One's supreme purpose flows from an all-embracing passion, mission, and vision. Finding personal purpose will include several of the following factors but transcends all of them. You cannot equate life's purpose with any of these unless you want to trivialize life and stray into random existence.

MORE THAN DESIGN AND FUNCTION

God has designed each of us in a particular way. But don't mistake specific design for purpose. Personal purpose will follow personal design, but it is not your ultimate purpose. If you go to patent offices, "designs have been registered before anything specific could be ascertained about their function, let alone the purpose of the functioning."[13] Often we discover personal design before general purpose. Just because there is evidence of design doesn't mean life's purpose can be found. Even atheists and nonbelievers can find personal design. Design can show specifics of function, but purpose relates to consciousness. Just because I function in a certain way (my design), function doesn't prove the purpose for my existence. For a universal, permanent, comprehensive purpose, one needs external justification and perspective. Specific design and personal purpose should not be confused. They relate to each other but should be distinguished. A bicycle possesses design and function. An abandoned bicycle evidences design but evokes sympathy. Even though it can be taken some-where, it cannot go anywhere by itself, on purpose.

MORE THAN GIFTEDNESS
AND TALENT

God gives talents to every human being, believers and nonbe-lievers alike. On that premise you possess at least one talent that is significantly yours. I hope your talent matches your vocation. I can't think of two ends of the talent spectrum more diverse than sales agents and accountants. Common sense keeps you from putting an accountant in a sales job and vice versa, unless you want to take a loss for tax reasons.

Further, God especially endows His children with spiritu-al gifts. If you are a Christian, you possess at least one spiri-tual gift that is specially and individually yours. The presence of special gifts and talents can help you with the upper level of the building of life, but your mission derives from your basic human responsibilities more than from your unique giftedness. Remember you can discover latent gifts, uncover specific gifts in larger clusters, and develop gifts into effectiveness as long as you live. But your purpose will always be expansive enough to include the discovery, deployment, and development of gifts. Your purpose will use your gifts but will exceed your gifts. Discovery of talents and gifts will aid the discovery of personal purpose and unique vision, but they are not identical to the grand, great, general purpose of all human existence. How many talented and gifted people are directionless! Just because a bike can go one hundred miles an hour doesn't mean it must be included in the race.

MORE THAN TEMPERAMENT AND PERSONALITY

How your temperament is constituted or cultivated does not indicate your general purpose. Even if you are designed with a particular personality and have enjoyed success in specific situations, you could as easily be "purposeless" as "purposeful." Super GT bikes used by the champions at the 1996 Olympics cost $30,000 to $70,000 apiece. No two bikes were alike—each distinctly created for its rider for maximum response. Yet these distinct and distinguishable bikes needed external purpose and energy to maximize their "temperament" and "personality." Further, those customized bikes actually adjusted to the styles and demands of their riders. Your particular vision and temperament will correspond to each other. Your temperament will be utilized in the grand purpose.

MORE THAN HISTORY AND EXPERIENCE

You already exhibit a specific history. Every day you add to your unique biography. Hopefully, you have learned from your experiences and from others' lives. Yet, personal history and experience must be viewed as useful for the larger purpose. Most minute experiences don't make for purpose. It's what you make of those experiences that relate to the particular application of your purpose. Since you are more than the sum of your experiences, your purpose needs to be bigger than the experiences. Further, your "experiences" have all been past or present. That's why it's called experience. Your future may look completely different. So, you shouldn't be stuck in what your past reveals, though for the foreseeable future you build your life on how the past has looked and on how the present is experienced. Your supreme purpose will be good for past, present, and future. To continue the bike illustration, each racing bicycle is unique in its experience. It may even have won the *Tour de France*. That's a statement of the past. Is there anything from past experience that can be inferred for present activity? and future involvement?

MORE THAN NEEDS AND DEMANDS

While human needs reveal the range of our necessary involvement and personal response, not all needs require involvement. Breeze through your newspaper today, and you'll find human needs galore—the homeless and the hungry, drug addiction and sexual diseases, educational and employment needs, family and marriage crises, political and economic upheaval—almost as many needs as there are humans. If you go beyond navel-gazing, if you aren't isolated by apathy or preoccupied with self-centered endeavors, you will be struck by needs. Some of these needs will never cease to seize you. Unless your sole purpose and soul passion are clear, you will be pulled and torn by human needs. Instead, you stand in need of a supreme purpose that is wider than human need, though that purpose will call you to turn some of these human needs into service opportunities. Does the need for a bike to go somewhere, to be ridden, to be "biked," ever justify its use? No.

MORE THAN GOALS AND PLANS

Your purpose will be implemented by goals and plans but is higher than these. Planning works with the details of how the purpose will look in personal mission and how your resulting vision will be accomplished in a lifetime, real-time. You may write out a goal or plan for applying your purpose—to finish a college degree, or attain one billion dollars in sales, or distribute ten thousand Bibles. But you cannot and should not confuse these goals and plans for life purpose. The future of a famed bicycle may be on display at the museum of a champion's hometown, but a strategy in how to accomplish that vision is not its purpose for existence. Even its supposed future history is not written in stone.

IS!

What is the intentional life? What should be life's purpose? What connects foundation, ground floor, and superstructure? *A supreme, soul purpose.* What bridges the gap between theology and practice, belief and behavior, verbal profession and personal embrace? *A supreme, sole passion.* Soul purpose and sole passion link head and heart, yoke professed belief and operational values. Before we use the rest of this series to construct life's building, we need to look at what *purpose* is. The following brief composite furnishes the outline we will follow through the rest of the book. You are still reading my introductory chapters!

FEATURES OF PURPOSE

Keep the upcoming definition clear so you won't confuse purpose with its ingredients. Current literature on business leadership and strategic planning often confuses purpose with mission and/or vision. Instead, *purpose is:*

> ➤ a permanent theme that affects every segment of life;

> ➤ the common link between any dimension of life; and

> ➤ an identifiable thread that weaves all parts of life—past, present, and future; internal and external; private and public; belief and behavior; motivations, attitudes, and actions; loves and duties; personal, family, work, and service life—into a single whole.

Purpose comprises a composite synthesis of the various elements of life.

INGREDIENTS OF PURPOSE

Since purpose is a composite, it contains several ingredients. Keep the following elements distinct, each of which will be further explained in upcoming books. Remember these are *distinctions,* not *divisions.* We cannot neatly divide them when they are found in the "ego agglomerate"—you. You are one person, though a complex one at that. Purpose comprises three integrated facets:

As the figure illustrates, *Passion* represents the foundation of your life. *Mission* represents the ground floor. *Vision* represents the superstructure.

> *Passion* relates to what you have set your heart upon; that which possesses, energizes, and unleashes you; your strategic *heartbeat,* the *élan vital* of life. It is your underlying purpose.

Mission relates to what you must do repeatedly, responsibly, regularly in life; your strategic *mind-set* in the business of daily life. It conveys your ulterior purpose.

Vision relates to what impact, difference, and change you are going to make in the world; your strategic *lifestyle*—that controls choices, determines usefulness, and pulls your profitability into the future. It distinguishes your unique purpose within your supreme purpose.

The above distinctions are not only inseparable but also function in a certain order or internal relationship. If you make your mission your foundation, you would end up being shallow and shaky. If you make your vision your foundation, you will build a huge edifice on slender support. If you make passion or vision your ground floor, you will neglect the matters at hand by quietistic withdrawal or wistful dreaming. If you make passion or mission your vision, you will enjoy the benefits of detached spirituality or preoccupied busyness. You need all three ingredients—passion, mission, and vision—to provide the compelling purpose of life.

BENEFITS OF PURPOSE

The supreme purpose provides several benefits:

- ➤ Unity for cohesion
- ➤ Totality for foundation
- ➤ Objectivity for dispassion
- ➤ Universality for inclusion
- ➤ Purity for clarification

- ➤ Security for self-possession
- ➤ Tranquility for submission
- ➤ Stability for consolation
- ➤ Identity for liberation
- ➤ Clarity for devotion

From these benefits, we can understand several features of the most appropriate human purpose. The supreme purpose, the compelling purpose, the ultimate purpose will be:

Single and expansive. It must fit the "one thing" category. If I were to say, "This one thing I am, I have, I know, I want, or I do," the supreme purpose will singularly manifest it. It will provide unity and continue to expand into the multiple dimensions of life. *E Pluribus Unum* ("out of the many, one") characterizes this single purpose.

Definite and intensive. It provides a positive definiteness, an identifiable statement to which we shall subscribe at every level of existence—foundational passion, ground floor mission, and unique vision. One's compelling purpose is not mere theoretical abstraction, though it can be debated and discussed at that level. It *definitely* claims and *intensively* rules all existence—head, heart, and hands, even the loins and feet.

Comprehensive and extensive. As mentioned before, purpose will apply equally

to all time: past, present and future;

to all dimensions: self, family, work, service;

to all aspects: thinking, feeling, doing;

to all activities: leading, loving, lingering;

to all motives: fear, greed, security;

to any person.

The supreme, compelling, ultimate purpose of life is singular, definite, comprehensive, expansive, intensive, and extensive. It carries the three integrated facets, the big sectors of human spirituality:

Passion—where is my heart-set for my love, trust, and sufficiency?

Mission—where is my head-set in my daily responsibilities?

Vision—where is my hand-set in serving a world of need beginning immediately?

"Find Purpose" screams the Tata Finance Group advertising billboard in proud national colors standing over the busy highway overpass in sophisticated South Delhi, India. South Delhiites exhibit somewhat snobbish attitudes and unimaginable amounts of discretionary income. That finance company's slogan actually puts right perspective in their lives. Unless you find purpose you will not use money wisely. I think they intended for us to borrow money from them to fund whatever purpose we find! They found *their* purpose of making money much easier if you found purposes to finance by borrowing their finances at above-market rates. Their point is clear; the object is confused. A purposeful, meaningful, intentional life beckons the entanglement of your heart, the recruitment of your soul, and the harnessing of your mind in worthy passion after a most excellent Object.

Profiling Passion

In A.D. 79, Mount Vesuvius doused the city of Pompeii with deathly lava. When she began to blow her top, there was enough time to escape from the city to safety. Instead, many people returned to their homes to retrieve what they were passionately committed to. Even in the face of danger they went after what they loved; what they hungered and thirsted after; what gave joy and enthusiasm to life; what was ultimately important to them. Doomed by delay, their lives were snuffed out.

> *Passion makes every detail important; there is no realism like the insatiable realism of love.*
>
> ❧G. K. CHESTERTON

Archaeologists discovered numerous well-preserved lava-mummies from the historic disaster. They found hands clutched close to breasts, fingers clenched tightly around objects that were obviously of great importance to the ancients. Once pried open, the hands revealed bags of gold—the supreme purpose for which they lived. They lived for and died for their passion.[1]

IDENTIFYING PASSION

In short, passion answers the question, "What do you love enough to die for?" Passion addresses the biblical issue of where you have placed your heart, your love, your trust, and your sufficiency. You can tell a person's passion by what he or she is willing to die for. What a person is willing to die for is what he or she is living for—the passion of his or her life.[2]

From the Greek root word for *path* (Latin *passio*) comes the Bible's primary use of the word *passion*, referring especially to the sufferings of Jesus during "Passion" week (cf. Acts 1:3 in old English, *American Standard Version,* and *Revised Version*). The biblical word can also mean "emotion" (cf. Acts 14:15; James 5:17). Today we use passion in the broad sense to mean "powerful emotion." Strong emotion can manifest itself in love, anger, or zeal. In contemporary use, passion often conveys "over-emotion," that is, inordinate affection (Col. 3:5; cf. Rom. 1:26), and heart-lust (1 Thess. 4:5). One recognizes "over-emotion" by asking, "What have I set my heart upon?"

Passion and *intentionality* are verbal and existential synonyms. Nobody follows passion unintentionally, or it wouldn't be passion. The first constituent of the intentional life, of the supreme purpose, is passion, for one chooses the ultimate object of his love. People choose what they are willing to live and die for, suffer and sacrifice for.

At the Himalayan Mountain Climbing Institute in Darjeeling, India (home of the world-famous teas), I encountered museum evidence of raw passion—men who set their heart upon climbing Mount Everest no matter the cost. I saw a pair of shoes made for stubbed feet. Bitten by frost, the climber's toes were chopped off. He waited to heal, ordered a pair of shoes for toeless feet, and then attempted to conquer the world's highest mountain. That's raw passion in all its defined intentionality.[3]

Passion contains a passive element as well. "What am I going to let affect me (the Latin root of *passion* means "to act upon") in such a way that I will sacrifice or suffer in order to achieve it?" By passion, then, we don't mean rage or fanaticism or infatuation in an arbitrary way. Terrorists focus on causes and hormone-heated teenagers focus on the opposite sex in that uncontrolled way, neither group counting nor caring for the cost of that passion. That kind of passion is really *impassion*.

A recent television commercial taunted, "Why does your neighbor, who makes less than you do, drive a better car and live in a finer home than you do? Well, that's simple," proclaimed the ad. "Your neighbor has borrowed easier and cheaper money from a particular financial services company that would be equally glad to loan you funds!" You too could then go after the same passions by borrowing money from them—a clear case of not counting nor caring for the cost of money.

True passion, instead, considers the cost but still pursues the object passionately. That kind of passion launches intentional living with core love permeating every part of life. Your passion gives you convictions about what is ultra-important to you, the criteria by which all of life is driven, gains energy, and continues. In passion you will find:

➤ extreme love for an object evidenced by abandonment to it

➤ intense commitment joined with exhilaration

➤ craving—hunger and thirst guided by a basic focus

➤ joyful enthusiasm chaperoned by adventurous involvement

Passion, then, is difficult to define, less hard to describe, quite easy to detect, and once discovered, easy to declare. The intentional life that pursues a supreme purpose begins with a demanding and commanding passion. Passion includes the following sub-ingredients.[4]

Passion entails an idea.

I like the French phrase *idée fixe,* a fixed idea, the heart fixed on an idea that is worth being fixated upon. "Nothing contributes so much to tranquilizing the mind as a steady purpose—a point on which the soul may fix its intellectual eye," said Mary Wollstonecraft Shelley (1797–1851). The preeminent idea demands a total fixation, a lasting, intellectual commitment. Passion without an idea produces a life at the edge of nerves and curves—thoughtlessly extreme. What is your stated (and state-able) passion?

Passion tends toward objects—worthy and unworthy.

It should be directed toward persons, for persons are of immense value. It is more right to direct passion toward people than things, to-do lists, possessions, and programs. Passion toward the supreme Person is the most appropriate for all passion. You don't want to merely love ideas, unless you hold unshakable tenure as a confirmed ivory-tower psychotic, with a drawerful of erasers of course, at the local university's arts and humanities department. The person and the idea that call for your passionate commitment cannot be separated. A passion without a person is heavy pursuit of a small purpose. With the highest Person, it is the heaviest pursuit of the supreme purpose. *Whom* may you love like that?

Passion requires a purpose, the supreme purpose.
Indeed, they are parallel and contiguous—the higher and stronger the purpose, the greater the passion that flows from and toward that purpose. The ultimate purpose beckons free and hot pursuit, vigor and risk, without debate and qualification. Such a purpose calls for life and, if necessary, death. That passion theme connects with historical understandings of the word—the double meaning referring both to the sufferings of Christ and to Christ's pursuit of the supreme purpose in which He fulfilled His passion.

The peculiar link between ambition and action (cf. Gal. 4:17) expresses one's *affections*. It is no wonder that Paul exhorts us to set our affection on things above (Col. 3:2) after declaring the supremacy of Christ and His work (Col. 1–2). From "above" Paul descends down to home, down to earth, down to life's responsibilities.

Where should Christians find their passion? From the endower of new life, the exemplar of new conduct, the energizer of new motivations, the empowerer of new action—the Lord Jesus Christ. Jesus brings "an element of intensity into the ordinary pursuits and activities of men."[5] That element of intensity derives from a passionate life after God. "I want to know Christ," declares Paul, "and the power of his resurrection and the fellowship of sharing in his sufferings, becoming like him in his death" (Phil. 3:10). Paul's declaration delivers the full force of personal passion. Setting your heart upon the Lord Jesus Christ, being affected by him, and therefore willing to serve no matter what the cost becomes our underlying passion—the radical, drastic, complete, total, out-and-out, ultra-passion toward God himself. What will be the driving force of your life until your last breath? Your answer to that question reveals your passion.

Passion exists within a worldview.

Passion exists within an appropriate cosmic framework, a worldview within which the person, idea, and purpose makes passionate sense. One's worldview addresses questions of personal origin, identity, meaning, destiny, and morality. These in turn will enable the discovery and nurture of the intentional life, the question of personal purpose and meaning.[6] Consequently, the person, the idea, and the purpose consumes you with intensity and joy, hunger and thirst, love and submission, zeal and activity. The "first thing" of all reality—chronologically first and existentially powerful—ontologically holds all reality together, cosmically and personally. What is it that solicits the hardest pursuit, which qualifies for the supreme human purpose? That first thing will serve as the foundation for the intentional life.

PASSION: THE FOUNDATION OF THE INTENTIONAL LIFE

These blast-furnace North Texas summers! They transform the color of grass into bronze. The sun occupies your living room. Cooperating with North Texas clay soil, they bring about many structural problems for houses. Living in North Texas, our family equates summers with dwelling dilemmas, just as people identify cities with crime. Like national anthems opening ball games, they seem to be causally related but are not particularly connected.

House deconstruction happens slowly. Hairline cracks on walls snake their way up to the ceiling. You touch up the cracks in a sort of cosmetic cover-up, but that doesn't help doors close properly. Soon after the surface rehabilitation, the cracks reappear. So you call on petty contractors to do some "taping and bedding" over the serpentine formations. But the walls crack again, testing the competencies of your only shelter, your dwindling bank account, and your patience quotient.

We saw cracks on the outside and inside, on floors and ceilings. Not only did they look ugly, but we also were warned that structural damage could make the house unlivable. The home wouldn't be fit for resale unless we undertook extensive foundation reinforcement. The back of our house, a recent addition, was pulling away from the main part. For six months we lived in two houses, an inch and a half apart, on one property.

My family gradually became amateur experts in foundation repairs. Don't rule out amateur experts. As the old line goes, "The Titanic was built by professionals, while Noah's ark was put together by amateurs." Profoundly affected by the discomfort and expense of our foundation repair, our seventh-grade son wrote a science paper on why buildings experience foundation problems. Complete with hypothesis, experiment, pictures, humor, and all. He called it "The House Cracker Experiment."

1. Do not water one side of your house for six to seven years.

2. After six to seven years, you will start noticing cracks in the corners of the walls and on your floors.

3. Six to seven years should give your dad plenty of time to come up with the huge amount to pay for foundation repair.

After constructing an experimental foundation of toothpicks and glue in plastic boxes, he concluded:

1. Foundations move and shift.

2. They fail because the soil around them expands and

contracts. Soils move causing tension to the foundations which in turn swell and shift.

3. Soils upheave because of moisture variations. When there is a prolonged dry spell, loss of soil moisture causes shifting of soil, foundation, and structure.

When soil expands, foundations shift, and eventually the structure fails. Similarly, I liken soil expansion to the environment in which you live. If life is not a fluke, it seems fickle, with an insecure tie to its foundation. Unless your foundation is strong, head-on collisions with erraticism erode the integrity and function of your life's foundation. Small and weak purposes will yield to environmental pushes and pulls as they collide with your principles and priorities.

External factors test the strength of the foundation. Soil expansion seeks to dislodge the building from the foundation. Your foundation shifts. The ground floor feels the moves. Soil presses in on you. In fact, your entire structure is set to unravel. Cracks are evident all over the place. You seem to be living in two dwellings—what you say is the foundation of your life and what you manifest in life. Life is pulling away from you. Your personal purpose is not integrally tied to your supreme purpose.

Finding and grounding your passion in purpose cannot be left to happenstance or circumstance. Left to luck, the supreme purpose tends to become whatever you make it to be for the moment. Even if you know what your ultimate purpose should be, your heart for life can fray, crack, and break if you pursue it haphazardly. Life's shifting sands, the natural pulls, the multiple demands, the daily routines, tighten a subterranean vise on you. They compete and collide against your life's foundation till you finally buckle under.

Like an aging wooden fencepost, your pointed top wears off, the shaft leans and eventually falls—unless the Intentional Life is sought, founded, grounded, and built.

The first thing in pursuing the Intentional Life is to take care of the First Thing—the foundation of your life. Yet another advertisement by a financial services company touted, "Be Your Own Rock!" Apparently, this commercial proposed, I could best demonstrate being *my* own rock by accessing *their* services. Of course, I wondered why I would need them if I were to be my own rock. Their encouragement to be my foundation actually laid out an irony. They exposed the flimsiness of a self-made foundation. If there ever was a feeble foundation, it is your Self. And your soul knows it very well. You've been founding your life on effervescent, insubstantial froth. Consequently, consider the very First Thing for your life-building enterprise. The First Thing of your life is not the first floor. Don't build that floor yet. The First Thing is your life's foundation, the first constituent of your supreme purpose.

FOUNDATION BASICS

The foundation concept evokes three major metaphoric identifications. First, it could be slanted to mean *source, origin,* and *beginning,* indicating a power that precedes and commences a series. This meaning is reflected in the Encyclopedia Brittanica entry on George Washington Pierce, "with his many influential publications on radiotelegraphy and electroacoustics, led to his being credited with building the scientific foundations of electrical communication." The meaning of foundation here relates to a past sense—of giving birth to, causing to be, generating something.

Second, foundation carries the undertone (intentional!) of the present *basis, ground,* and *underpinning* of a structure.

The structure may possess a foundation, but the foundation needs to be laid on a rock stratum. A house of cards does not possess a foundation in this sense. Without a proper foundation there is no stability. The rock is the final, ultimate ground in the laying of a foundation, which in turn governs the structure's quality in an ongoing way.

Third, the foundation concept connotes a *directing, conforming,* and *guiding* of the future. The kind of foundation civil engineers lay depends on the weight of the building yet to be constructed—design drives foundation-laying and building. Sometimes the dimensions of the building are restricted by the foundation that has already been laid—here, foundations drive the design. Medieval Mughal architecture in northern India evidences delicate balance and beauty, but Shah Jahan (the builder of the Taj Mahal) could not afford to build beyond the symmetry that foundations allowed. In this sense, foundations control the future. For instance, when we say that "the foundation of democracy is individual freedom," we go beyond the sense of past origins and present sustenance to the future. Representative democracy originated, is sustained, and will be directed from this foundation.

THE FOUNDATION OF ALL
FOUNDATIONS

Unfortunately, with the rest of humanity, you and I face a foundation problem. Subsoil conditions in life are not favorable for laying a secure foundation. Humanity lost its moorings very early in our history. You may know the biblical account. The Bible says that we crashed at the Fall. We were created to relate to God, to reverence Him, to reflect His glory on the earth. Instead, we fell. We missed the right mark and we hit the wrong mark. We assumed God's function upon ourselves. We decided to be our own rock. And God didn't like human assertiveness very much because it revealed our quicksand nature.

Humans fell from God's expectations into themselves and have been failing ever since. Just as a fallen tree cannot erect itself back up, we are stuck and unable to help ourselves. Thrown out of an immediate relationship with almighty God, humankind has been falling since that first, devastating spiritual earthquake. Every one of us is spiritually quagmired. Each time a life enters the world (at present, sixty-two thousand daily in India alone; 114 million annually around the globe) the Fall begins anew. Each of us begins spiritually fallen and stuck. Unless we are resurrected and supernaturally changed from our deathly state, it will be unwise to build anything on us. We are dead in our wrong behavior, in our trespasses, in our transgressions. Separated from God, we can't make a single move that merits His favor. Our best shots, to use a basketball analogy, are "air balls." Yes, we can walk on quicksand—quickly. But it rolls and shakes under the smallest weight, and anything that stands still is swallowed up. Nervous, shaky, and with a limited destination in view, we perform admirable balancing acts. However, we can't provide a foundation. We can't be our own rock.

If we examine the loaded idea of foundation, it also communicates "function"—creating, undergirding, determining. It symbolizes "principle"—fundamental, rudimental, and directional. It also portrays strength, stability, and consistency. Think now of what it takes to be the foundation rock, to function like a rock, for life, for humanity, for all reality. Whom does it take to restore the solid basis on which we may build life? Who can bring fracturing walls together and "feather out the swell"? Who will rejoin cracks? Unarguably, the answer is GOD. God fits any and every sense of the word *foundation*. God is the only one who qualifies as a comprehensive foundation—the causative, carrying, and commanding power—for human life.

God, according to the Old Testament, lays the foundation for everything. He set the earth on its foundations (Ps. 104:5), has marked them out (Job 38:4–6; Prov. 8:29), and owns them (1 Sam. 2:8). He is able to hold these pillars firm (Ps. 75:3) and to shake the earth off its foundation (Job 9:6). In these verses, God, the foundation of everything, impresses us with His independence, ownership, and power. Neither the earth nor humankind can be our foundation. He is the foundation of foundations and lays the foundation of all life, including yours and mine.

The New Testament uses two words to communicate this profound foundation concept of God as the foundation of all foundations. *Katabole* means "beginning, that which gives something direction and determination."[7] The Creator's work, rights, and attributes hover over this word. He is the creator-founder-director-determiner, and is therefore the foundation of everything created. The second word, *themelios,* carries the physical analogy.[8] "The durability and toughness of a building depends on the quality of its foundations, and the same is true of human life. *Themelios* connotes this basis, usually not obvious to the observer, which upholds, supports and affects the whole edifice."[9]

God in the Bible, then, is that kind of foundation of all reality. The Bible clearly commends the Lord Jesus Christ, God's only Son, as the foundation for an individual's life. The Lord Jesus Christ qualifies as the foundation for human life by virtue of being God. How is this divine foundation link to Jesus established?

According to Paul, Jesus is the First Person—before all things. First in chronological existence (Col. 1:17), in ontological existence (Col. 1:15), and in creative activity (Col. 1:16). Paul says, "God was pleased to have all his fullness dwell in him (Col. 1:19; cf. 2:9). Therefore, all that God is, Jesus is. He was before all things. He created all things. The Bible says that not only is Jesus God, as the First Person (the beginner) of reality, He is the First Person of present, ongoing reality—"in him all things hold together" (Col. 1:17)—the director and determiner of present reality. Jesus is *katabole!* You, as part of reality, need to relate to Him as the founder-creator-director-determiner of your life.[10] You, as a part of reality, need to make Him the stratum on which your personal life's foundation can be laid—your *themelios.* Again, the apostle Paul speaks of Jesus being the only and true foundation. "For no one can lay any foundation other than the one already laid, which is Jesus Christ" (1 Cor. 3:11). Jesus is the bedrock on which you can build with the right or the wrong materials, but there is no negotiating who the bedrock is.[11]

How can Jesus become the bedrock of your life? If you have not embraced Jesus as the bedrock of your life, you must immediately deal with the critical issue that separates you from God, the founder and foundation of all reality. Your self-reliant, self-oriented, self-created ways of saving yourself, of being your own rock, cannot be trusted anymore. You have to change your mind concerning who your foundation will be: your Self or God-Jesus? Trusting yourself for meaning and purpose is sin. Sin separates you from God. Therefore, God constructs a bridge to overcome the separation. A well-founded bridge, with one end in deity and the other end in humanity, spans the gap between God and you.

That crossing place, that connection, is Jesus. Jesus as God's bridge is the foundation, the beginner, director, and determiner of your eternal salvation.

In a "foundational" verse on foundation—that eventually points to Jesus as the foundation for human life—God presents the way to salvation: "The one who trusts [God's sure foundation] will never be dismayed" (Isa. 28:16). If you trust Jesus, you will never be disappointed. You will be saved from your Self, from your sin, and from your spiritual separation. The way to God will be open again for you. Then God, in Jesus, becomes the foundation for your life. He will then become your rock and your refuge.

Have you trusted the Lord Jesus as your only Savior from lostness, rootlessness, and foundationlessness? From sin? Jesus became God's pier-and-beam foundation for all people in history and geography. God laid a new Creation foundation for all people, a stratum wide enough and strong enough to hold everybody who wants to build his or her life on a solid rock foundation. For those who are like fallen trees because their roots are not embedded in underlying support, God provided it.

The new foundation and provision for rootedness was laid in human time by Jesus. Indeed, God erected a "tree" as a symbol and instrument to provide the underlying support that our lives require. A tree can represent the biblical picture of the cross—the tree on which Christ died (Gal. 3:13). By dying on the cross-tree, Jesus attacked the root cause of human foundationlessness—sin. He Himself became sin itself: "God made him who had no sin to be sin for us, so that in him we might become the righteousness of God" (2 Cor. 5:21).

When our son Ryan was in third grade, he developed the bad habit of getting his name on the board at school. Taking after his father, he talked a bit too much and too loudly. He collected demerits. Each day we reviewed his transgressions, evidenced by his name on the teacher's board. Each day he resolved to do better. We tried everything from cajoling to candy. From extended reasoning to deprivation. No tactic stemmed his behavior. I eventually resorted to spanking in an attempt to underscore the seriousness of his offense. He cried before the spanking, during the spanking, and after the spanking. Yet the board again featured his name. What could we do?

One day, in desperation, I announced to him that if his name appeared on the board the following day, he would get to spank me. He wept at that statement. He understood the seriousness of it. He knew someone had to pay the price for the violation. Next time it would be his dad. He decided that night to not get his name on the board.

We both left for school the next morning. All day I thought about my beloved son. Would he get his name on the board? If he did, would I follow through with the reverse spanking? My students were quite interested in this strange twist to the parenting process.

At 3:00 P.M., I called my wife to see if his name had materialized on the board. Alas, it had turned up. I rushed to a hushed home that evening. Ryan was quiet, not still, but milder than usual. We ate dinner. He and I walked to the bedroom. We again talked about how serious this offense was. Somebody had to pay the price, the penalty for his misbehavior. This time it would be me. I went through humiliation as I unbelted my trousers, dropped them, and laid over the bed.

"All right, son, it's time for you to spank me."

"I can't do that, Dad!" he wailed.

"Someone has to pay for the wrong, son. Go ahead and spank me."

Wracked by emotional turbulence, he raised his hand a few inches high and dropped it gently on my seat.

"That's not how Daddy spanks, son. You need to spank me, actually spank me."

"Dad, how could I do that?"

"But someone has to pay the price, son. Go ahead."

He raised his hand a bit higher this time, though it felt limp on my backside. When I thought the message got through, I got off the bed and dressed. We both went on with life. For some reason, Ryan never got his name on the board again. Oh yes, he made some other mistakes, but we didn't have to deal with this problem again. We noticed those new demerits, talked about them, but there was no need to spank him on the primary issue anymore. The price for his demerits, past, present, and future, had been covered by his dad.

If an eight year old spanking his dad for minor infractions seems irrational and imprudent to you, another payment for sin was far more ludicrous. God tried to get our attention for the error of our ways in so many ways. He covenanted with the human race, He blessed and disciplined us, He cajoled, commanded, and condemned us. Nothing made us understand the seriousness of our offenses against His greatness and holiness. Nothing got us to change. Finally, He incarnated Himself into time-space living conditions. He lay on a cross, disrobed in humiliation. We spanked Him. We wanted to. He died.

On the third day, He got up. Up from the dead. Now dressed and ready, He serves as the foundation of our new life. He wants you to relate to Him, not only as Creator-founder but as Savior-lover, the One whom you subjected to a horrendous spanking. When you trust the Creator-founder to be the Savior-lover of your life, you have grasped the First

Thing in finding life's ultimate purpose. Christ becomes the new foundation in your life by repentance and faith (Heb. 6:1).[12] You must change your mind about building on the wrong foundation, the acts that led to death. Instead, you must lay the foundation of faith in God. Repentance and faith cannot be separated at the foundational level. You may now leave the foundation of death and move on to God, the foundation of life. One morning a bumper sticker on the car in front of me caused me to pause with a query, "Do you *really* know Jesus?" I had to go back to the time when I transferred my trust to Him. I could really say, "Yes! Yes, I *really* know Jesus." I don't know Him as well as I would like to, could, or should. But I *really* know Jesus.

Let me ask you, "Do you *really* know Jesus?" If you can't point to a time when you deliberately trusted Him to be your only God and Savior, you can respond to Him right now. Wherever you are. From the caverns of your soul, as honestly as you can, talk to Him. If you are not sure that Jesus is your eternal Savior, speak to Him. Tell Him, "Lord Jesus, I need You for my foundation. I have trusted myself for too long. I want to accept Your way of salvation as my own. Thank You for addressing my sinful separation by dying instead of me on that cross. Thank You for taking my spanking. Thank You for giving me hope for the future by rising from the dead. I invite You to be the foundation of my life, its efforts, its desires, and its activities, by becoming my Savior from all that separates me from You. Be my *katabole,* my *themelios,* my foundation."

Listen, my friend, God is not only the foundation of heaven and earth, of His people in the Old and New Testaments, He becomes your foundation, the Savior, lover, director, and determiner of your life. He also will be the ongoing strength of your life, the foundation for the *first* floor you need to build. He will become your underlying purpose, the support for the higher floors, the passion you need to build for your unique mission and vision through life.

In the book of Colossians, we saw Jesus' qualification as our Savior and foundation repairer. There we also find His continuing foundation presence. Our relationship with God has faith in Christ as its foundation (Col. 1:23). From now on, our lives must be rooted and built up in Him (Col. 2:7). Jesus, according to Paul, is to be a full-function *themelios* in our lives. The foundation for our eternal life and earthly life, future life and present life, relational life and task life, is the Lord Jesus Christ. Beginning straightaway.

Jesus is the stratum rock of salvation on which you must lay your foundation. Our connection to the foundation is established by personal salvation through Jesus. We get connected through a crisis moment by which we are saved—in the past-tense sense. As foundational source and origin, He began the salvation process. You finally transferred your trust to Him as your only Rock. Here and now, in the present-tense sense, in an ongoing manner, He functions as the exposed rock on which your columns will be laid. Jesus becomes the bearing stratum. To address the subsoil conditions of humanity's continued rebellion against God, it took the strength of Jesus and His cross to bring us a firm salvation foundation.[13] That is the very First Thing of the intentional life.

Salvation-foundations need to be secure, indestructible, unshakable.[14] By personally trusting the Lord Jesus Christ as your only God and Savior, the rock is unearthed for life's building needs. The Creator's strong foundation can give us the consistency, firmness, and stability needed for first-floor and upper-level construction. On Christ, the solid foundation, we can build anything, for anything. Jesus' foundational role in your life is secured by His eternal salvation. It is also possible to be sustained in present existence by that foundation.

"History demonstrates the folly of building a huge edifice . . . on slender foundations."[15] We must build on the rock. Lay the right foundation. Architecture and design sources tell me that a building needs a bearing-pile device to transmit the load of the building to the rock. Solid materials for bearing piles are either precast concrete or steel. Archaeologists have examined the foundations of many a building from ancient times. They can even decipher the outlines of the superstructure because what was attached to the bedrock has survived. In the same way, we too need to lay some bearing piles to carry our life's load down to the rock. Your foundation rock secures your salvation. But we must lay a foundation on the rock with the right materials. Or, if your foundation has shifted due to hostile subsoil conditions, we need to undertake some foundation restoration.

How can we pursue a well-built, long-lasting house, a life that is well-grounded and well-purposed? I point you to the basic action—laying the right foundation, or for many of us, restoring life's foundation to original design, intent, and quality.

Reinforcing Passion

An entire village in the Philippines gave chase to a thief who went alternative shopping at the local department store. With no escape in sight, he climbed up a coconut tree. Villagers shook their head in dismay at this vain climb. First they thought they would wait it out as the moron contemplated how long he would stay up there.

> *A most ingenious architect had contrived a new method of building houses, by beginning at the roof and working downward to the foundation.*
>
> —JONATHAN SWIFT

Then came the start-up sounds of a chain saw. They sawed off the tree at the bottom. The thief fell to his death.

In his pressure to escape, the thief overlooked a fundamental feature with reference to trees. Unless a tall tree stays connected to the earth, it can't provide security. The earth is immovable, but the tree is saw-able. The thief was a double fool—morally deficient and practically incompetent.[1]

Moral and practical ineptitude form the basic components of the biblical word for *folly*. Too many Christians are fools. A "Christian fool" should be a verbal oxymoron, but unfortunately we find them in action all over the place. The brilliant pastor who falls into adultery and justifies the ongoing relationship is a Christian fool. The religious mother, tired of caring for her family, who abandons her husband and kids to "find herself," is a Christian fool. The Christian kid who crucifies his parents by his rebellion is a Christian fool. Any time we break God's Word we are fools. Too many Christians who began building with Christ as their foundation rock in a saving sense have been living life without Christ as their sustaining foundation. Like the thief above, they and you have been climbing up the wrong tree. You have gone up but can't come down. Chain saws rev up each day to undercut your existence. Your tree sways at the lightest gusts. A life-crash begins. If Jesus is the un-saw-able, unshakable, eternal foundation, why are we not laying and living our lives on that foundation rock? Because believers, instead of being wise people, can be "fool" people.

At the climax of His Sermon on the Mount (Matt. 7:24–27), the Lord Jesus narrated an evocative story about laying the right kind of foundation on which to build one's life. Luke's version (6:46–49, NASB) of Jesus' words read:

> Why do you call Me, "Lord, Lord," and do not do what I say? Everyone who comes to Me and hears My words and acts on them, I will show you whom he is like: he is like a man building a house, who dug deep and laid a foundation on the rock; and when a flood occurred, the torrent burst against that house and could not shake it, because it had been well built.
>
> But the one who has heard and has not acted accordingly is like a man who built a house on the ground without any foundation; and the torrent burst against it and immediately it collapsed, and the ruin of that house was great.

COMPARED LIVES

The Great Teacher compared and contrasted the two men in a most insightful parable. These life-builders were alike in external, temporal ways. Both built a house. "Building a house" is simply an analogy for the "building of a life."[2] You don't have to do much to build a life. Check your pulse. If you are alive, you are building a life. You may not resemble a well-designed house, but you do represent a living construction site. The results may not yield a lasting structure, but you function as the building contractor of your life.

Some build elaborate lives. News media are filled with the famous, powerful, and monied of the world. Their lives remind me of the Sand World exhibit at the miniature city, Madurodam, outside The Hague in the Netherlands. Sand World presents a huge, elaborate display of the story of the Netherlands, produced using 700,000 kilograms of sand.

Building a sand sculpture of this magnitude involves a complicated process. Layer upon layer of sand is deposited into a wooden mold. Each layer is watered and thoroughly tamped down. The hard compacting process gives the structure its strength as each mold adds to the pyramid shape. Then comes the carving and shaping. Once the top layer is completed the next mold down is removed. Thus the carvers work from top to bottom until the entire structure is completed. Once the work is finished, there are no molds left. The top can no longer be reached, which is why the carving at the top must be perfect from the start. For all its details and massive size, the Sand World sculpture requires careful protection from the elements. A few minutes of hard rain would wreak havoc on that elaborate project. Both the men in Jesus' story "built" their lives. Even while setting up for a hard crash, we can "build" lives.

Both builders heard Jesus' words. The foolish man did not lack information or guidance. The wise man and the foolish man knew what Jesus had said. They were part of the multitudes (Matt. 5:1) who heard Jesus firsthand. They already knew His expectations. They might have even professed they knew Jesus' words. For most of us, too, our problem is not a lack of knowledge.

Both men experienced storms in life. Storms and suffering never practice discretion. They strike at all people in the most unexpected moments. Storms do not discriminate between wise men and fools.

The 1997–98 El Niño weather pattern ranks as one of the worst in international memory. It took many forms in Latin America, including drought and fire, storm and flood. El Niño swept away roads, bridges, homes, farms, lives, and livelihoods. It actually created a vast lake in a north Peruvian desert. No one knows why it happens, but every year around December— that's why the name El Niño, the Christ Child—a warm Pacific current flows east to the coast of Ecuador and Peru. We know the mechanisms, but the root cause eludes us. Satellite observations and new weather buoys now enable a fierce El Niño to be foreseen months in advance, though no one knows in what form or where the extremes of weather will strike. Amusingly, in December 1997 the leading news weekly in Brazil, Veja, recommended 1998 as the perfect year for a northeastern holiday, since El Niño promised "an exceptional season, with lots of sun, blue sky, warm water, and soft breezes." Storms arrived to blow away their desired expectations.

Wind and rain rarely visit the towns on the Pacific coast of Mexico. Yet they experienced downpours and had to build dikes, clean waterways, and strengthen bridges. In 1997, June's flash floods in Chile made 80,000 people homeless.

Topsoil washed away while huge waves eroded beaches and raised salt levels in coastal farmland. Polluted floodwaters resulted in cholera, diarrhea, and other intestinal diseases.[3]

We too can expect trials, anticipate struggles, and experience storms as part of a fallen world. We live among imperfect people on a groaning planet. Marital struggles, financial stresses, relational strains, and weather disturbances strike everybody, whether wise or foolish.

CONTRASTED LIVES
The two life-builders were alike in external ways but they were *unlike* each other in the following critical, internal ways.

Character
They differed in character: Jesus calls one a wise man and the other a foolish man in the Matthew 7 passage. A fundamental quality of wisdom characterized one and was absent in the other.

The wise man was not simply an information man possessing extraordinary brains, or a data man with extraordinary memory, or even an educated man who was arrogant and untested. He applied the knowledge he had. "The trouble with the information age," one article observes, "is that it seems to place no value on differentiation. . . . Perhaps, the rate of increase of information, and even of knowledge, has not been matched by the rate of increase of wisdom."[4] For instance, John Forbes Nash Jr. excelled as a mathematical genius, graduated from Princeton University with a skinny twenty-seven-page doctoral dissertation on the theory of competitive games, and later gained the Nobel Prize. He eventually produced "one of the most important pieces of mathematical analysis in this century,"[5] relegating his

Nobel-winning work to triviality by comparison.

Now read about Nash's wrong-headedness in piecemeal summary. During the same period of technical accomplishment, Dr. Nash had two homosexual relationships that left deep emotional scars. He managed to get arrested in a sting operation in Santa Monica, California, which cost him his summer consulting job at the Rand Corporation. He took a mistress whom he treated with casual, selfish cruelty but who bore him a son. By the age of thirty, he had begun his inexorable descent into madness (cf. Jesus' word "fool" here). He married a beautiful, aristocratic Salvadoran named Alicia Larde, a rare female physics major at MIT and had another son, John, named after himself. He resigned his tenured position almost as soon as he received it, tried to give up his American citizenship, managed to get himself expelled from both Switzerland and France, and suffered a series of involuntary hospitalizations that put him at the mercy of psychiatric crudities like insulin shock therapy. He made himself unwelcome by going into restaurants barefoot. With shoulder-length hair and a bushy black beard, his face wore a fixed expression, a dead gaze. Women, especially, found him frightening. Although he and Alicia were divorced in 1963, she took him back as a boarder in 1970 because no one else would! Though brilliant in intellect (the movie version of his story won four Academy awards in 2001), he wasn't a wise man in Jesus' terms. He could still become one.

"Flagpole sitters" also fail to apply wisdom. In 1992, Frank Perkins of Los Angeles attempted to beat the world flagpole-sitting record. By the time he came down, eight hours short of the four hundred-day record, his sponsor had gone bankrupt, his girlfriend had left him, and his phone and electricity had been cut off! Who wants to distinguish himself in this idealistic and isolationist sense? Such people remove themselves from the complexities, confusions, and conundrums of life. We salute their commitment but question their judgment. Isolationists are better at pontificating from privileged safety than living real life.

Instead, in Jesus' story the Greek word for a wise man—*phronimos*—refers to the type of person who "considers well what he is about and carefully adopts measures suited to his purpose. The undertaking on hand is building a house—a serious business—a house not being meant for show, or for the moment, but for a lasting home."[6] He builds his life—intentionally. He is practically wise, not just pragmatically savvy. He is rational and realistic, prudent and practical, full of sense and sensibility. He chooses to build on the rock foundation, the source of his sensibility. A foundational wiseness characterizes him. He is a person everyone can be. The obverse of the wise man is the wise guy, the "fool-man." The latter is (also) a person everyone can be.

Let's look at the fool-man's character. Jesus used the word "moron" (a transliteration from Greek), which refers to the dull, stupid, and foolish. In the Bible, folly is the antonym of wisdom. The moron's profile originates in the Old Testament. "It is not imbecility, insanity, or error. It is *wrong-headedness*, having to do with practical insights on the nature of things that lead to success or failure in life. Wisdom and folly in the Bible rest on alignment and adjustment to a higher principle for a practical purpose. Folly involves rejection or disregard of the revealed moral and spiritual values on which life is based. The fool sins against his own best interests and rejects God (Ps. 14:1) [italics mine]."[7]

The fool's very nature is foolish or "wrong-headed." He is headed in the wrong direction at increased speed. The traffic reporter this morning called some drivers "morons"—

they knew better. For them, it was not an issue of knowledge. They didn't act on what they knew to be right and true—wrong-headed morons. Taxi drivers in New Delhi are notorious for their suicidal impulses. A green traffic light stands for "go." Orange means "go faster." They keep on going when signals turn red. To curb these self-destructive tendencies, the police have actually painted the word "relax" on red lights. One driver bragged as he broke another traffic ordinance: "Do you know why Indian taxi drivers are the best in the world? Because we are not afraid to die." I sweated the ride, confessed all my sins, and became a firm believer in an Islamicized Calvinism—the arbitrary, autocratic sovereignty of God. Moronic drivers know the wisdom of the rules but intentionally neglect them. They think wrongly about the right direction.

Notice that the two men in the Lord's parable are not characterized as wise and foolish by the kind of foundation they chose. They already possessed an innate character that directed their choices of the foundation on which to build. Their choices identified them as wise or foolish. Further, it wasn't the storms that made them wise. The storms simply revealed what they already were.

I recall flying into Seattle, Washington, in 1983. Compared to most countries, immigration and customs proceed rather easily in the U.S. This occasion, however, was different. I was quizzed, frisked, and searched. They checked my bags for concealed weapons in my toiletry kit, hand baggage, and computer case. They knocked on my hard-back suitcase to see if it had a false bottom. Then the security agents had the audacity to ask for my wallet. They went through my driver's license, credit card, alien registration card, and insurance card. My business cards intrigued them, especially those with writing on them. Were names, addresses, and phone numbers of contacts hidden there? Surprised by their search, I finally dared to ask them about their sudden interest in my life. "Well," said the officer, "the Indian Prime Minister is arriving later today. There have been threats on her life. The whole world is on a security alert, and we needed to thoroughly check every passenger arriving into the U.S. with an Indian passport during her stay here."

I understood their action. The violation of my privacy revealed something about me to security officials. Their examination didn't make me upright—just uptight. It only revealed to them what I *already* was on the inside. Their inspection proved my character. Similarly, the storms didn't make the wise man wise and the foolish man foolish. Storms revealed what they already were—wise or foolish.

Authority

The two men differed in authority: one heard and acted on Jesus' words; the other merely heard Jesus' words. The wise man valued Jesus' words enough to act upon them. He built on the rock foundation (Luke's emphasis) and laid the right foundation for living (Matthew's stress) on the rock.

The foolish man, however, heard Jesus' words but didn't act accordingly. He didn't value them enough to align himself to Jesus' teaching. He did not make Jesus his authority. He did not adjust to Jesus as the higher One. He was a fool because he sinned against God's recommendation to let the rock foundation control all of life. He sinned against his own best interests.

Think about it. Wherein lay his foolishness? The fool-man didn't deliberately go about laying a wrong foundation. That would be a rebellious person—another word in Scripture to suit unbelievers. "Moron" fits believers and unbelievers. He just didn't take thought of building on or laying the right foundation at all. Unfortunately, a sand foundation is a foundation that is not really a foundation. The foolish man identified the foundation by listening to Jesus. But he didn't want his life to connect to Jesus, to build on the foundation, to install the bearing piles. It wasn't a problem of two foundations—the foolish man really had no foundation at all.

There is a fool who has said in his heart there is no God (Ps. 14:1; 53:1). But the Christian fool who knows better is worse off. He has heard but he doesn't apply. He reveals the fool's gap between his life and his profession, knowledge, and behavior.

An encyclopedia definition states, "All foundations must transmit the building loads to a stable stratum of earth. There are two criteria for stability: first, the soil under the foundations should be able to receive the imposed load . . . and, second, the settlement should be uniform under the entire building." The Christian fool may have located the stable stratum of the earth—Jesus as the rock foundation. But he hasn't laid the right foundation on the bedrock. The problem with the Leaning Tower of Pisa has nothing to do with the structure itself—the builders simply laid the foundation in sandy soil.[8] The fool-man's foundation is not appropriate or uniform to the load of his life. It is unable to transmit the load to the rock. The soil under his life is not able to support the load, nor is the settlement uniform. Any other foundation than hearing and doing Jesus' words will be uneven, causing displacement, damage, and even deconstruction.

So the two men were different at the level of qualitative character traits—wise and fool. They were different in their authoritative values—one valued and laid a solid foundation; the other laid a stupid foundation. The latter was wrong-headed in not considering foundation issues. The final difference between wise man and fool-man comes in the wake of the storms.

Outcome
These two construction projects resulted in drastically different outcomes. One man lived and left a lasting house. The other just lived and left. One built a house that survived the winds; the other built a house that blew away. A well-built life depends on a well-laid foundation. The longevity of your spiritual life-building depends on the quality of your foundation-laying exercise. The bedrock may be strong, but if you don't lay a good foundation on that rock, your life remains susceptible to the storms. Your house will surrender to the winds. Any structure you put up will succumb to the elements.

The wise man's life survived the storms. After the storms were done with the wise man's life, his house still stood. It did not fall, for it had been founded upon the rock (Luke 6:48).

I spoke at the Financial Club in Jakarta, Indonesia, to the elite of an industrious and illustrious nation, during a very difficult time in their economic history. The spring of 1998 brought on monetary pressure of catastrophic proportions. Not a single bank was solvent. Their currency lost 30 percent of its value in one day. Even those completely debt free were suddenly 30 percent poorer, paying interest on money that they didn't borrow. Our hosts expected three hundred people on that muggy, summer night. Soon, three hundred fifty had signed up to come to a banquet hall that could only hold three hundred. I was told, "Economic storms make them more sensitive to spiritual matters." Spiritual hunger made them forgo a sit-down dinner to hold a "stand-up" dinner to accommodate everyone. I arrived at noon on the meeting day and four hundred twenty had registered. They had to cut off registration. We prayed that many would cancel that night. Fortunately, some did. Just before I spoke, an Indonesian businessman gave his testimony. A well-known person, the head of an 800-billion rupiah company (at R40=$1 that spring, that's $20 billion), he was a knowledgeable man. His Christian witness demonstrated that he was a wise man too. A few weeks prior, he had lost his Managing Director position (roughly equivalent to CEO) of the mega-company. He said, "Ladies and gentlemen, you know my story. You have been following it in the newspapers and seen my face on television. I am here to tell you, the Lord Jesus was with me when I was on top; the Lord Jesus is with me when I am at the bottom."

I thought, there stands a wise man who built his house on the rock. He is surviving the storm. I am not sure how long he will be unemployed. I do know that his life has stayed past the immediate stress. His house did not fall down. Why? Because "it had been founded—passive state of completion in the past. It had been built upon the rock and it stood."[9] He possessed foundational strength.

The foolish man's life was smashed by the storms. Jesus simply says, "And it fell—and great was its fall" (Matt. 7:27 NASB). Compare the two accounts to grasp Jesus' graphic statement of the moron's plight. The house of cards collapsed instantly. The ruin was complete. When a foolish man's life crashes, everyone can hear the thud. Foundation strength and stability were missing, but not because the foolish man didn't know the right foundation. The foolish man had even called Jesus "Lord."[10] The fool-man knew the right foundation, only he didn't consider it when building his life. He didn't attach his building enterprise to its strength. He didn't give it authority and power over his life. Why anyone would hear and not do Jesus' words points to the connection between a qualitative personal trait (foolishness) and valued authority (foundation). A fool does not derive his authority from God's words and is overwhelmed.

HEARING AND DOING

Certainly, the disjunction between hearing and doing is not a new problem among believers. A standard dilemma from the very beginning of the Christian faith, listen to the apostle James' words, and then act on his instruction.

> Do not merely listen to the word, and so deceive your-selves. Do what it says. Anyone who listens to the word but does not do what it says is like a man who looks at his face in a mirror and, after looking at him-self, goes away and immediately forgets what he looks like. But the man who looks intently into the perfect law that gives freedom, and continues to do this, not forgetting what he has heard, but doing it—he will be blessed in what he does. (James 1:22–25)[11]

How will we be blessed in what we do? According to James, by hearing and doing God's Word. How does one lay a foundation on the rock? By hearing and doing Jesus' words. How will we survive the storms of life? By hearing, then doing what Jesus said.

Hearing His words is necessary for Jesus to be one's *theme-lios,* one's rock foundation. Jesus' words, in this context, explicitly refer to the Sermon on the Mount and later to all His teaching (cf. Matt. 28:20). Implicitly, Jesus' words refer to the entire New Testament, for the rest of the Bible was recorded by the reminding ministry of the Holy Spirit to the apostolic authors of Jesus' teachings (John 14:26). The classic verse on divine inspiration (2 Tim. 3:16) carries a similar foundational and extensive thrust. God-breathed Scriptures were given to lead you to salvation through faith in Christ Jesus (2 Tim. 3:15)—Jesus is your foundation who saves you. But the Scriptures were also inspired to instruct, rebuke, correct, and train you in righteousness (2 Tim. 3:16)—the continuing foundation for life. That verse primarily refers to the Old Testament since some New Testament books had not been penned at the time of its writing. Yet the same Holy Spirit who in-breathed the Old Testament was also the One who reminded the apostles in their New Testament writings and inspired it. To hear Jesus' words, then, is to hear Scripture's words, because Jesus' words point to Scripture as His words. In John 2:22, written after the resurrection of Jesus, the disciples recall what He had said and make an amazing observation: The words of Scripture (the Old Testament) and the words that Jesus had spoken corresponded to each other! So we must *hear* the Scriptures in order to build on them.

However, hearing Jesus' words is not enough. We must live by those words. My son's recent interest in golf—that time-draining menace of a game—demonstrates the difference between knowledge and reality. He reads about golf, visits pertinent Internet sites, and looks up the rules. He plays golf computer games. He vicariously lives the lives of professionals. He mimics perfect swings. He has worked through introductory manuals. But he hasn't yet played a round of golf at the time of this writing! As of now, my son hasn't swung a golf stick, a club, or the axe yet. Does he know golf? No! He has read about it, heard about it, spoken about it. But he doesn't know it. Because part of the reality of golf is in doing it. Knowledge is not power. Knowledge draws power from application. Doing gives reality to hearing.

The foolish man hears Jesus' words. But he must *practice* or build his life on Jesus' words to experience their reality. Putting them into practice gives power to the rock foundation in the context of life. In short, a person must embrace Jesus— His work for salvation, and His words for one's foundation— to build a sturdy life. The foundation must not only serve as a foundation on which to build but a foundation by which to live. The foundation provides the substructure but also defines the superstructure. Christianity—embracing Jesus—is not only the way to life, it is a way of life. Here is a comprehensive, consistent, competent worldview by which we live on the earth. It is not a theoretical tapestry of ideas as found in religious philosophies. Jesus Christ authorizes the way of life. His message is complementary to life, carrying directions and benefits to life. Jesus' message, heard and lived, makes wisdom a reality in your life and mine.

Connecting Passion

A businessman owned a warehouse that sat empty for months and needed repairs. Vandals had damaged the doors and smashed the windows, and trash was everywhere inside the building. When the businessman showed a prospective buyer the property, he took great pains to say that he would replace the broken windows, bring in a crew to correct any structural damage, and clean out all the garbage.

> *The best time to plant a tree*
> *was twenty years ago;*
> *The second best time is now.*
> *—CHINESE PROVERB*

"Forget about the repairs," the buyer said. "When I buy this place, I'm going to build something entirely new. I don't want the building. I just want the site."[1]

In the same way, the Lord Jesus didn't want the life-building you had constructed. It had lain empty, neglected, even vandalized over many years. You couldn't clean out the garbage, let alone repair it. Jesus bought your life for a price (1 Cor. 6:20), and you have given Him access to your site. Together you are building something new from the foundation up.

The site has been bought and prepared; the foundation has been found and laid. Now, starting immediately, we can yield control to the new Owner's designs for life and build according to His values by connecting foundational passion with life-building.

THE ROLE OF VALUES

A person's values bridge the gap between belief and behavior, knowledge and action, hearing and doing. People do not really do what they say they believe; they pursue and apply what they value. Value-drivenness is not so much a prescription to adopt but is simply a description of the human condition. You can tell what a person values by what he or she does, for values ignite imagination, inform decisions, and drive actions. A mutual give-and-take between values and action continues throughout life. Values must guide action, and they already do.[2] On the one hand, we must "subordinate an impulse to a value," as Stephen Covey suggests.[3] On the other hand, all people are driven and controlled by values that provide the foundational principles for their lives.[4] The fool in Jesus' parable displays his values by building on a sand foundation. The wise man's values originate in his attachment to the rock foundation—moving from hearing to doing, from philosophy to practice, from idea to action. His life increases in compatibility, alignment, and harmony with those values.

The question, then, concerns our values, for our life is built not just on beliefs and ideas, but on a person, the Lord Jesus Christ and His values. We need a correspondence between Jesus' teachings and our values. If the person of Jesus Christ is our foundation, the teaching of Christ provides the source and framework for our value system. In short, the central control console of our lives—our biblical worldview—must form a foundation of values to translate into the governance of our lives.

THE BEATITUDES AS VALUES

In this section, we will examine the Beatitudes as a controlling paradigm for life's values, attitudes, and posture. In context, the Beatitudes are part of the same sermon whose concluding story of the wise and foolish men we expounded in the last chapter. The Beatitudes serve as one brilliant summary of Jesus' words that we are to hear and put into action. They furnish a framework for a life of good works in response to the groundwork of God's work in our lives. Below I would like to demonstrate a process to help you move from being a foolish person (simply hearing) to a wise one (hearing and obeying). In it you will also find a method of Bible study that, when utilized, will claim your ongoing obedience.

Viewing the Beatitudes as simply ethical principles outside their theological backdrop is to reduce them to a common human ethic. Other religions propound a version of the Golden Rule. Some see the religions as offering negative versions ("Do not do unto others what you would not have them do to you") with only Jesus proposing the positive version. Mahatma Gandhi clearly subscribed to Christ's ethic of love, for "to repay an eye for an eye leaves every one blind." It is not known that Gandhiji personally received the Lord Jesus Christ as his only saving foundation. Yes, the Beatitudes provide a brilliant ethical set for life. Even non-Christians (witness Buddhist monastic approximation of compassion, humility, etc.) will benefit from applying these guidelines.

The Beatitudes, however, offer us much more than a set of bare ethical guidelines. If we follow them within the theological framework of the Lord Jesus Christ as our personal foundation of salvation, the Beatitudes will maintain compatibility between beliefs and behavior. Since He founded a comprehensive and coherent worldview, His teaching is also complementary to living. Educators and sociologists say learning that transforms must be learning in the context of action *(praxis)*. Abstract, detached, theoretical knowledge is as useless as impulsive, unprincipled, pragmatic action. The Beatitudes complement life. So they guide those who wisely seek compatibility between faith and practice, hearing and doing, orthodoxy and orthopraxy.

How do we go about being and becoming wise? By bringing truth to bear on life.

The wise person *transliterates* God's expectations into core values. He then *translates* them into strategies for obedience. The first action acknowledges the timeless authority of God's Word; the second acknowledges the timely practicality of God's Word.

However, just because he states core values and comes up with a plan for obedience does not mean he turns them into reality. The wise man also intentionally *transfers* those strategies into reality.

This reality-transference strategy answers three questions:

➤ *What* does Jesus (the Bible) say? The truth to be transliterated.

➤ *So what* does it mean to my life? The application to be translated.

➤ *Now what* do I do in obedience? The strategy to be transferred.

As you read the section on Christian core values, study each Beatitude with a pencil in hand, intending to address it at these three levels—a rudimentary attempt at becoming wise.

CHRISTIAN CORE VALUES
(MATTHEW 5:3-10)

I consider the Beatitudes as core values in the sense that Jesus differentiates the disciples from the multitudes, doers from mere hearers, wise people from fools, by their response to the Sermon on the Mount. Multitudes hear, but only the disciples accept the criteria for the blessing of and functioning in Jesus' kingdom. As the introduction to the sermon, the Beatitudes follow the rule of first words as weighty words. These are priority statements of core values for disciples, traits to be true of those who live with God's kingdom agenda in mind with special reference to King Jesus. In Middle Eastern imagery, speaking from a mountain (hence, the Sermon on the *Mount*) attributed kingly authority to the speaker. After the Resurrection, Jesus met His disciples on the *mountain* and commissioned them (Matt. 28:16–20).

Jesus, as authority, clearly exerts kingship rights on His followers. He pronounces blessings on those who live by His values in contrast to the multitudes who are merely interested in what He has to propose rather than in living by His authority.

The increasing authority of Jesus arising from His foundational role in one's life will include these values. Let me lead off with a more complete treatment of the first two beatitudes and pare off the extent of my help in *your* exploration of this passage for the rest of the beatitudes. Remember the *What does Jesus say, So what does it mean to my life,* and *Now what do I do* questions as you consider these prompter statements.

Blessed are the poor in spirit, for theirs is the kingdom of heaven (v. 3).

What? The core value here is of *dependence on God.* While the unqualified "poor" in Luke fits that author's emphasis on the economically destitute (cf. 6:20), Matthew's version refers to anyone whose only hope is in God. It is no surprise that those materially deprived trust God more. Those who can't control the environment, or predict the circumstance, or seemingly generate their future—usually found in economically weaker countries—simply must depend on God more. So one's dependence on God may arise from circumstantial deprivation. Self-dependence, often sanctioned by earthly advantages of wealth, status, and power, works against poverty in spirit.

Neither poverty nor riches can get you into heaven. But riches can keep you out of the kingdom—an obstacle that poor people don't contemplate before considering God. Jesus' condemnation of the Laodicean church precisely addresses human self-sufficiency: "You say, 'I am rich; I have acquired wealth and do not need a thing.' But you do not realize that you are wretched, pitiful, poor, blind and naked" (Rev. 3:17). Yet God-confidence must arise from a variety of factors that emphasize our inability and inadequacy in life. The poor in spirit acknowledge their contingent status. They are not passive, indifferent, or haphazard but instead rely on God for all of life. They acknowledge the true foundation of their life as the foundation of all life.

So What? "Dependence" is not a good word in the two cultures to which I belong—my birth land of India and my adoptive land of America. Both nations value democratic freedom. Though surrounded by cultural justification of unlimited freedom, I am called to the biblical value of dependence. I must depend on God and not be diffident with him. My dependence acknowledges my innate inability to mimic or please him. When it comes to God, I am inferior in every way—in ability, morality, and status. My poverty in spirit indicates a poverty of spirit. My awareness of my deficiency grows in the realization that in spite of personal spiritual pauperism, God accepts me.

Since I am spiritually destitute, I must empty myself of the temptations to function as sovereign over my life. I must yield in the many implications that flow from self-deification. I must submit to His authority. I must depend on His direction. When I function like God, I am self-sufficient in spirit. Instead, poverty in spirit recognizes the impotence of my goodness ("all my righteousness is like filthy rags") and my achievements ("counted as dung") as I stand in utter indigence before almighty God. My outer sophistication is sophistry. To possess the blessings of the kingdom of heaven I must acknowledge my ongoing disqualification from the kingdom. I am impotent in spirit, impoverished in soul, indigent in life. My ownership of a piece of the kingdom requires God's salvation of my life. That salvation drives my soul's passion toward my Savior.

Now What? I daily check my tendency to be my own resource in addressing my own spiritual bankruptcy. I cannot merit God's blessings by pharisaically routinizing my life with good works to manipulate His favor. I look into my life to discern where I operate out of my supposed strengths—the discipline of Bible reading, journal writing, public ministry—and recognize them as irrelevant in terms of possessing God's kingdom. Even when functioning in the areas of God's gifts to me, I will enter each opportunity with dependence on God. I will baptize each ministry with prayer. I will also seek opportunities that expose my limitations so I can abandon myself to the mercy of God's provision.

I will continually rediscover the meaning of dependence— I can't do anything significant without God. Indeed, without

Him I can do nothing profitable or produce anything fruitful for eternity. But I enjoy His rulership in life as I continue to acknowledge my internal bankruptcy before Him. I confess my arrogance, I concede my dependence, I cry for His sustenance. Each day I get out of bed flying the white flag of surrender at full mast. I will not relegate God to emergency situations. He will exert ongoing influence over the mundane and the momentous issues of my life. I must build the core value of God-dependence in every aspect of life, so my boldness in life comes from abandonment. My courage must originate in Him.

Blessed are those who mourn, for they will be comforted (v. 4).

What? This Beatitude records the core value of *brokenness before God.* Think of Jesus' paradox here. No one in his right mind would equate "blessedness" with "brokenness." Jesus seems warped in the value He places on mourning, because we distort the meaning of blessedness. We assume that blessedness means "happiness," and we confuse *well-being* with well-feeling.[5] But *well-being (blessedness)* and *well-feeling (happiness)* are possibly competing conceptions! Well-feeling describes a psychological conception of happiness. Well-being can include well-feeling but not vice versa.[6]

Jesus' use of "mourning" primarily relates to moral mourning. Grief over sin, sorrow for transgression, and anguish over displeasing God. Personal sin plays a huge part in defining the human problem within the Christian theological setting. Mourning fills a significant biblical component of confession and repentance. Mourning, because the smallest sin is interpreted in comparison with the infinite magnitude of a perfect God. Sorrow, because the very principle of life from which Jesus rescued us is deliberately given power when we sin, and thus demeans divine provision. Regret, not so much for getting caught but over sin in its essence as mutinous, a slap on the face of God.

Brokenness exhibits dismay, disappointment, and anguish. Psalm 51 shows a full-blown expression of interior brokenness by David, the superpower king of that age, and encourages us in our own mourning. He came unglued as he realized that his defensive rationalizations were sin as well. He sinned against God and God alone. He desired truth in the inward parts so that everything that had been lost could be reanimated by God.

So What? If brokenness is a core value for my daily living, I must modify my concept of happiness. Happiness is arbitrary and temporary; blessedness is a wholistic[7] assessment of one's life. It is more than well-feeling. It is well-being, a life well lived, an appraisal of the totality of life in its various dimensions. This means I may not be "happy" at a particular moment in my job or period in my marriage, but the overall appraisal of my job or marriage is one of blessedness, even desirability. Blessedness is wholistic and totalistic in its reach.

Further, when it comes to anguish over personal sin, my brokenness becomes a prelude to blessedness. Sin disrupts. It carries on its chicanery as an intruder. Sin severed human relationship with God at the beginning. It continues to break the human-divine relationship. This time, we must break one break with another—brokenness and confession overcomes the break between us and God. How do we experience brokenness of heart and contrition of spirit?

> *By rejecting defensiveness.* Attempts to explain sin sound like excuses to God. After all, He can think of better explanations and excuses for my sin than I can.

> *By recognizing sin as sin.* I am an artist at rationalization and cover-up. I use everything from Satan to

orching summer heat to justify my moron-ism.

By repentance. By changing my mind concerning the value of a particular sin in my life.

Brokenness rightly responds to God's breaking of our wills, to God's storming our lives.

Now What? I take regular comfort in the psalms, repeating the chants of the crushed, reading the Bible of the broken-hearted. "The LORD is close to the brokenhearted and saves those who are crushed in spirit" (Ps. 34:18). "The sacrifices of God are a broken spirit; a broken and contrite heart, O God, you will not despise" (Ps. 51:17). Brokenness motivates clarity of mind and thought. "Tremble, and do not sin" (Ps. 4:4, NASB).

I confess one specific sin to God each day, assessing my closeness to God by how specific my confession gets. I find that the more general my confession, the farther I am from God. Conversely, the closer I am to Him, the more heinously specific my confession becomes.

I will give the Cross ongoing power in my life to bring me to brokenness:

for blood cleansing from sin,

for reminders of the cost of sin,

for motivation to keep from sin,

for help in forgiving myself.

God remembers my sin no more (Isa. 43:25). Will I? When was I last pierced in my heart about flagrant violation of God's expectations? When did I last weep over sin—my sin or another's sin? How recently have I been filled with godly sorrow? In 2 Corinthians 7:8–10 (NASB), a significant passage on the working of sorrow toward comfort, Paul writes,

For though I caused you sorrow by my letter, I do not regret it; though I did regret it—for I see that that letter caused you sorrow, though only for a while—I now rejoice, not that you were made sorrowful, but that you were made sorrowful to the point of repentance; for you were made sorrowful according to the will of God, so that you might not suffer loss in anything through us. For the sorrow that is according to the will of God produces a repentance without regret, leading to salvation, but the sorrow of the world produces death.

Brokenness leaves a life without regret over regret. It brings on the consolation of God in divine forgiveness, fellowship, and nearness. It also leads to discovery of areas of weakness, opportunities for strengthening, and edges to be smoothed out. I am blessed enough to build spiritual brokenness into my value system. Spiritual brokenness protects a life from truly breaking.

Blessed are the meek, for they will inherit the earth (v. 5).

What? A key value of the kingdom is *meekness before God and others.* The scope of this powerful word goes from unpretentiousness to freedom from pride, all the way to exhibiting patient gentleness.

Wrong views of meekness abound. Meekness cannot counter the drive to be known as humble. Neither is it the inability to act confidently. It is definitely not timidity, which bespeaks weakness and shyness. Meekness is the Self, succumbing to itself as it cultivates a true estimate of itself in relation to other selves. Meekness is clearly not thinking too highly of ourselves. But it is not thinking less of ourselves; *it is thinking of ourselves less.* Indeed, meekness focuses on others, their needs, and their quirks. Meekness receives all that humility offers, with strength. Instead of pretension, it presents authenticity; instead of vengeance, self-control; instead of impatient anger, strong gentleness. While dependent (Matt. 5:3), the disciple is not passive; since he or she is meek, the disciple is not aggressive. For those who wait long enough, the future kingdom on earth becomes their guaranteed inheritance. Only the meek will wait that long.

So What? Meekness as a personal value contests everything that gives me self-value! There is pleasure in revenge, but meekness calls for surrendering the right to retribution. Irritability during busyness often reveals a self-inclined heart, but gentleness allows an unchangeable irritant to inculcate patience in my life.

Meekness builds on the value of humility. God resists the proud, and I don't want God against me. If God is against me, I can't build a life on Him. Therefore, in what areas of my life do I find meekness lacking and pride lurking? Am I really meek or simply timid? What about false humility?

Former Israeli Prime Minister Golda Meir reportedly chided one of her generals, "Don't be so humble. You are not that great!" Where can I pursue authenticity before God and others? God already knows my pretense, but have I worked hard at faking sincerity and succeeded in fooling others? Where do I consider myself superior to others—in position, in endowment, or in any other way? When is pride legitimate? On the surface it seems like meekness disallows justifiable pride, but pride actually relates to feelings of superiority. When I rejoice in an accomplishment—mine or my child's—and don't feel haughty, I am being justifiably proud. However, anything that smacks of snobbishness cannot function as a foundational authority in my life. Value meekness!

Now What? Consider some strategies for pursuing meekness, humility, and gentleness in your life. For a starter, write out verses against pride ("Pride goes before a fall"; "God resists the proud") on an organizer to remind you each day of your propensity to harshness, pridefulness, and control. Just beware: the moment you become aware that you detest pride, you may fall into the pride of hating pride. Our minds are complex, but pride, the first sin, is even more so. Lay out some personal approaches to gentleness and meekness.

Blessed are those who hunger and thirst for righteousness, for they will be filled (v. 6).

What? Yearning for God's righteousness characterizes the disciple in the core of his or her being. Without valuing the yearning itself, we will be less than satisfied with satisfaction. Part of the satisfaction is the craving. Those who experience abundance do not relish abundance as much as those who crave satisfaction and then receive the blessing.

Hungering and thirsting after God characterized the psalmist's longing for God, "My soul thirsts for God, for the living God. When can I go and meet with God?" (Ps. 42:2); or, "O God, you are my God, earnestly I seek you; my soul thirsts for you, my body longs for you, in a dry and weary land where there is no water" (Ps. 63:1; also Ps. 143:6). Jesus' authoritative statement against the pursuit of the arbitrary, temporary, and ephemeral as our ultimate cravings fits the Beatitude. Instead, "Seek first his kingdom and his righteousness" (Matt. 6:33).

We could discuss the object of our longing—God's righteousness in personal salvation or enacted in society—but whichever it is, there is satisfaction in doing it wholeheartedly, devotedly, enthusiastically from the inside out. The disciple longs for personal and social righteousness and does what is necessary to facilitate and effect them. Of course, he yearningly waits for the kingdom, when righteousness will be culminated in its fullest sense in all dimensions and levels.

So What? We truly hunger and thirst for God but assuage that yearning with a thousand substitutes. We create alternative religions every day for satisfying our souls. Family, friends, food, hobbies, shopping, revenge, politics, hospitality, work, pleasure, and money—all compete with God as the single, absolute satisfaction for life. Unless we intentionally recognize their relative worth or worthlessness, they usurp God's place as God and dispute God's function as our soul-satisfier. Have we come to the place in our Christian journey when we unqualifiedly declare that God is enough, that we prefer God to anything else?

Having become righteous, made right with God, through faith in Christ, how may I cultivate a hunger and thirst after God, His kingdom, and His righteousness? What attitudes must I develop in the intermediate time, between now and the time the kingdom arrives in full righteousness? How should I contribute to social righteousness in order to approximate what God values for all people? As a participant in God's covenant community, the church, how could I enable the church to preview in snippets what kingdom righteousness will constitute in effulgence some day? How will I long for God's righteousness to be evident in me, in others, in the world?

Now What? It's your *turn* to *turn* the application into obedience—perhaps the first evidence of yearning after God's righteousness lies in this activity. Write a couple of specific, time-date stamped steps to reflect life-building on the value of craving for God.

Blessed are the merciful, for they will be shown mercy (v. 7).

What? Valuing mercy or compassion as a character trait of the spiritually wise person reflects *what has already been done in our lives.* We attach worth and value to mercy as a foundational component for vibrant, spiritual sustenance. Since God has been merciful, we are awake, alive, and alert today, physically and spiritually. We too then will show mercy. Mercy is extending what God has extended to us in our need. He also promises mercy for those who approach God's throne with confidence to find mercy and grace in time of need (Heb. 4:16). When we are merciful, we shall obtain mercy.

So What? Explore the application of this character trait as a core value in your life. What does "mercy" mean in terms of human need? What evidences your sensitivity to those less fortunate than yourself? How do you extend forgiveness to those who have offended, betrayed, or hurt you? Probe these angles for absorbing mercy into your life.

Now What? Your progress toward wisdom will be measured not only by the truthful way you answer the above questions but also by the specific steps you take to put those answers into action.

Blessed are the pure in heart, for they will see God (v. 8).

What? Purity in heart before God shows *transparency before God*—transparency that translates into internal honesty before God and in the undivided priority given to His kingdom. Kingdom priority on the outside is matched on the inside with cleanliness and truthfulness. Seeing God was the first desire of the "seers" of the ages. It may be the primal desire of all humanity.

A cab driver in Chennai, India, gave every evidence of

being a Christian. He displayed a Bible on his dashboard—an unusual feature in a predominantly Hinduistic land. To confirm his salvation, I asked the well-known evangelistic opener: "If you were to die and go to the entrance of heaven tonight, and God asked you why He should let you in, what would you say?" He replied in humble clarity, "I'll say, God, You should let me in because I've been waiting to see You all my life. I want to see Your face." Purity of heart receives the blessing of seeing God. Did his answer confirm his salvation? The desire to see God may cause him to consider what it would take to become pure of heart, which would in turn lead to the fulfillment of an otherwise frustrated desire to see God.

So What? It's time to translate the "what" of inner transparency into personal application. Am I clean and clear on the inside? Am I clear on Who makes me clean? What am I hiding, from whom? How much would I like to see God?

Now What? Make explicit some action points to integrate transparency into your life. Begin by asking God to point out impurities so you can intentionally allow Him to deal with them.

Blessed are the peacemakers, for they will be called sons of God (v. 9).

What? Peacemaking identifies the value of reconciliation, bringing understanding between enemies, former friends, and neighbors. Such efforts will cause people to recognize your godly heredity and lineage—a son or daughter of God. Look up the word *peacemaker* in a dictionary and Bible reference tools. Write out your expanding understanding.

So What? This project is entirely yours under the leadership of the Holy Spirit in application. Where to practice peacemaking? People needing reconciliation with God. Marriages you know which are breaking apart. Church splits. Tribal or racial reconciliation needs.

Now What? Under the correction and motivation of the Holy Spirit, identify areas of opportunity for you to initiate reconciliation. Ask God to make you sensitive to peace vacuums.

Blessed are those who are [and have been] persecuted because of righteousness, for theirs is the kingdom of heaven (v. 10).[8]

It is your turn to pursue all three levels with this final blessing. *What* is the foundational value stated here? *So what* does it mean in your life? *Now what* should you do with this character trait of the kingdom?[9]

The above exercises not only provide you with foundational insight and direction for action, they also lead you step-by-step through a process you can use when handling any part of God's Word. A wise person transliterates truth to relevance, translates relevance to applicability, and transfers applicability to obedience. Transliteration plus translation plus transfer leads to life transformation. This is the life that lasts beyond the immediate and final storms.[10]

UNDERTAKING A RECONSTRUCTION

When the Christian men's movement was highly visible in the United States, I was privileged to speak at several of their larger events. One year, my feature talk dwelt on "rewriting your epitaph at midstream." A doctor who heard God's Word that day decided to act on it. He shared in a highly lucrative business partnership. His problem, however, involved the frequent practice of abortion at their medical facility. He decided that prenatal murder was not "acting" on the Word he knew. He applied his knowledge, his hearing, his profession of Jesus' name, to his business life. He decided to give his salvation foundation the kind of sustaining, controlling power it rightly should play in his life. At the expense of income, power, and fame, and at the risk of his future, he went back to his city. He declared his valued conviction to partners who bought him out. He now runs a small medical enterprise at the low end of the monetary totem pole. This doctor *heard* and *did*. From a foolish man, he is transformed to a wise man, who lays and builds on the right foundation.

Continual foundation reinforcement is the wise choice of the wise person. It involves knowing, applying, and acting on God's revealed life values. Increasing submission to the Lord moves us from stupidity to sensibility; from instability to solidity; from wrong-headedness to right-headedness. Foolish men climb up saw-able trees when they should be digging deep and laying a foundation on the rock.

In summary, remember the First Thing of life to be taken care of relates to your salvation. You located Christ as the stratum rock, the rock on which to build your life. But the rock is not the superstructure. Some of your structure has already been built. Now you have to do the wise thing—to examine and reinforce what has been built by laying the right foundation on the rock. We have yet to sketch the biblical blueprint for the rest of your life. Whatever happens, don't put up another floor without reinforcing the foundation. Your life will easily disintegrate into randomness, be bantered by monotony, and shrivel by busyness. Not because the foundation *rock* has proven inadequate, but because you aren't increasingly applying the counsel of God to give that rock the authority to govern your life.

When Jesus spoke the parable of the two builders, several images could have emerged in His hearers' minds. Some would have thought of the elaborate ceremony in the ancient Middle East accompanying the laying of foundations. Laying a foundation showed a deliberate earnestness on the part of the builder to get the building started. Human sacrifice at foundation-laying events demonstrated the seriousness of the endeavor (cf. Josh. 6:26; 1 Kings 16:34). Huge feasting and celebration followed the ceremony.

Others in the audience may have contemplated the future angle of Jesus' story. That aspect compels an immediate decision from you. An eschatological storm—"the mother of all storms"—is going to touch, try, and test all people. Matthew uses a future passive tense: the wise man "will be[come] like." "The future tense is significant: the one who puts Jesus' words into practice will become like the man who . . . on Judgment Day, when the great storm comes, will stand fast because of his good foundation."[11] Luke emphasizes the present. Matthew's parable is decidedly futuristic. Jesus' future in Matthew points to the narrow way, which leads to life (7:13–14). Mere verbal profession doesn't get you into the kingdom. Building on the sand will demolish you. A tornadic cleanup of the world will reveal the true quality of your life. The big storm's a-coming (cf. Ezek. 13:10–13) to demonstrate whether you were a wise man or fool-man in this life. Will you survive that day?

It is really time for you to re-lay the foundation of your life. If you have strayed from Jesus as your foundation, dabbled with sand foundations, immersed in some other authority, it is time to re-lay your foundation with joy and earnestness for the present (Luke's emphasis) and future (Matthew's angle) in a celebrative, ceremonial style. You may want to invite those close to you to this public rededication event of life, will, and the future. You will show your commitment to building a legacy, an Intentional Life, a life that will survive any storm. For too long, you lived off the security of a life saved from eternal hell.

If you invited Jesus to be the foundation for life (perhaps even since beginning this book), I commend you. Surviving into that eternal future is critically important for the rest of your existence. However, you want to implement a survival system that lasts through earthly storms as well. These difficulties are immediate and viscerally experienced. Storms shake us to the core. Will they demolish us? According to the Lord Jesus, to wisely build an unshakable life you have to embrace Him in all of life. Will you embrace the reality of Jesus' grace? We can draw power from the Rock which saved us.

Are you giving authority to the Rock that saved you? By intentional embrace? By hearing His words and putting them into practice? There is no wisdom in trusting Him to be the First Person–creator of your salvation and not trusting Him to be the constant-sustainer of life's dimensions. He is already your saving foundation. He will be a continuing foundation when you hear His words and practice them. Become wise. Understand and obey. Know and apply. Draw a line in the sand, *really on the rock*. Will you stand on the side of wisdom or foolishness? Build on your salvation with wisdom, for by wisdom is a house built (Prov. 24:3). When you choose the path of Jesus' words—hearing and doing— you may claim stability, sturdiness, and staying power.

We now can go on to building the rest of the house on the First and Wise Thing(s)—the necessary and sufficient foundation for life—the Lord Jesus Christ.

Soul Passion, Sole Passion

Neil Armstrong symbolically conquered the moon for all humanity on July 20, 1969. My mother woke this thirteen year old at 4:00 A.M. that day in Southern India to listen to historic words discerned among the whistles and crackles of a shortwave radio transmission: "One small step for man; one giant leap for mankind." As urban legends go, after those earthshaking, planet-shuddering words, NASA scientists allegedly heard Armstrong whisper: "Good luck, Mr. Gorsky." They asked him to identify Mr. Gorsky, but he refused to tell. They pored over NASA records but found no one by that name. They checked Russian space logs for a Mr. Gorsky but no one turned up.

> *Once it was the blessing,*
> *now it is the Lord;*
> *Once it was the feeling,*
> *now it is His Word.*
> *Once His gift I wanted,*
> *now the Giver own;*
> *Once I sought for healing,*
> *now Himself alone.*
> — A. B. SIMPSON

Supposedly it wasn't until 1989 that Neil Armstrong finally revealed the meaning of his "Good luck, Mr. Gorsky." He and his brother played catch growing up. When Neil missed the ball, it invariably landed in the Gorsky yard.

While surreptitiously retrieving the ball one time, he heard Mrs. Gorsky barking at her husband like a seal. "Love? You want love? I'll tell you when you'll get love. When that kid next door walks on the moon!"

Love. That's soul passion in a word. For what a man loves, he will follow. What a woman values, she will obey. A person will live for and die for what he or she really loves. For Christians, God is to be our ultimate love, our only passion. Unfortunately, that kind of love toward God seems impossible. Fortunately, conversion's blessings root us in the God who makes the implausible plausible, the improbable probable, the impossible possible, even inevitable. Passionate, devoted love for God is not difficult; it is downright impossible. Unless we are seized with God as our passion, too many little loves compete for God's value and conflict with God's place in our lives.

The godly life, defined as ongoing passion toward God, is impossible. We do not contest its impossibility. The following questions illustrate the dilemma we face:

➤ If the godly life isn't impossible, why do we want to do what we shouldn't do? Why do we not want to do what we should do?

➤ If the godly life isn't impossible, why do God's expectations differ so radically from human points of view? He wants dependence; I fly flags of my own colors. He wants me to mourn over sin; I seek to rationalize and blame someone else. He wants me to be sensitive to others' needs; I prefer the selfish life.

➤ If the godly life isn't impossible, why does the Bible seem to be so impractical and unrealistic?

➤ If the godly life isn't impossible, why do God's commandments seem so burdensome and wearying?

My daughter, age eleven, assuming that professors do profess something, asked me what I profess as a professor! I listed three subjects I was teaching that semester, described the two technical ones, then told her the third was about the "Spiritual Life." I asked if she understood that subject.

She nodded, "Uh-huh!"

I probed, "What is the spiritual life, honey?"

She deferred to me, *"You* know, Dad!"

I pursued, "Yeah, I think I know what it is, but I want to find out what you think it is."

In childlike, unprohibited brilliance, she remarked, "It's the God-life!"

THE GOD-LIFE

I liked that answer. The spiritual life is exactly that—the God-life. The passionate life involves living the God-life, life for God, life by God. At the foundation-laying event of salvation, the very life of God—eternal life—entered us. Now we must live out that very God-life, building on the foundational framework. We can't build beyond what the foundation permits.

We can and will work out what God has worked in us. Obstacles will arise, for an ongoing residue—a natural capacity called the self-life—contests God's life in us. Consequently, the spiritual life proves impossible to grow, nurture, and cultivate—by *ourselves*. We can transliterate truth to beliefs, and translate beliefs into action points, but it takes a vital relationship with God to *transfer* truths and beliefs into foundational values and first-floor activity.

As one would expect, since God has designed the process, we possess the greatest resource for life building, soil preparing, and foundation maintenance—God Himself. "He who began a good work in you will carry it on to completion until the day of Christ Jesus" (Phil. 1:6). "For it is God who works in you to will and to act according to his good purpose" (Phil. 2:13). The godly life is a God-thing, life oriented around God. But the spiritual life is also God's thing. God is able to bring you faultless and flawless into His presence one day (see Jude 24).

You are not left alone to tend or monitor your spiritual foundation. Our house foundation repair company left ongoing maintenance to us, to our initiatives and our resources in soil moisture control. In the spiritual scheme, however, God is as concerned about your spiritual life as you are. In fact, He is more enthusiastic about your vitality than you are. Further, He specializes in making the impossible—your eventual perfection—inevitable. The maintenance of a spiritual foundation, the making of a godly life, remains an impossible God-thing in your life, but it also remains a possible God's thing in your life. That "God-thing–God's thing" correlation relates to the foundation's framework by which we live an intentional life. You can possess the finer insights of biblical truth, the good intentions of obedience, but if there is no motivation to realize them in life, you will still be a moron, building on sand.

THE FOUNDATIONAL COMMANDMENT

I would like to summarize the spiritual life by asking you to consider the foundational commandment. The first and great commandment illuminates passion for God. Mark 12:28–31 (also found in Matt. 22:34–40 and Luke 10:25–28) provides the framework of the foundation on which we build and by which we live. There we find Jesus' own expectation of spiritual passion, even a definition of the spiritual life. He delineates what is most important and most impossible in an ongoing relationship with God.

Living the God-life, you will love the Lord your God with all your *heart, soul, mind,* and *strength.* Godliness is a God-thing. Godliness is orientation to God, increasingly adjusting to His foundational lordship, because as Jesus says, there is only one Lord God, "the Lord is one" (Mark 12:29). Godliness is a God-thing.

The Lord Jesus then strings a set of words rehearsing Deuteronomy 6:5. Faithful Hebrews repeated that verse, the Shema, several times each day. Since values control us, Jesus addresses spirituality at the value level, the foundation of love. Again, whatever we love controls us. Our affections command us. Our values consume us. Remember, we don't do what we say we believe. We do what we value.

Love is one of those words that we understand intuitively and immediately, though if asked to define it we would be at a loss. A most elastic word in any language, we now use it for almost any object: "I love pizza. I love football. I love my computer. I love my family. I love Lucy. I love New York, Cape Town, Costa Rica," and so on.

Instead, love for God is a specific, special kind of love to be reserved for God alone—unselfish love, unlimited love, and unconditional love. Before we explore the dimensions of passion, evaluate whether you love God like that. Check the soil condition around your foundation with the following questions:

> ➤ Whatever your plans for today, the weekend, the month, the year, if Jesus came back today, would you be sad or glad?

> ➤ If God told you that you would never get to sin again, would you be disappointed? (I ask myself that question often in order to keep aligned to God's values concerning sin. Hard soil encroaches around my converted but crusty soul-foundation.)

➤ If the Bible disappeared from circulation and the Holy Spirit was removed from the earth, how soon would you miss their presence and empowerment in your life? Would others be able to tell you had strayed from the foundations of Christian living?

➤ If God told you that you didn't have to sacrifice anything to be of use to Him, that you could pursue your life without Him, how would you struggle with that announcement?

These questions represent a sample soul-soil check. If your answers revealed a hardened, dry, and cracked heart, they also revealed a critical level of need to attend to your values. That's why I emphasized Jesus' values in the last chapter. But the values of Jesus without love for the person of Jesus will turn into platitudes at best and into legalism at worst. It is the God-life that can transform those values into the motives and actions of God-love.

Remember, however, that the God-life in us is contested by the self-life, a life made up of our own agenda, preferences, and independence. The self-life stands in conflict with the God-life. The only way to break the tie between the God-life and the self-life is to address it at the level of our love-life. That's why Jesus speaks to you and me at that deep level. If our appetite is for God, He will control us. Jesus calls you and me to *love Him for who He is, with all you've got.*

LOVE THE LORD YOUR GOD

Why did Jesus begin with "Love the Lord your God? Because God is neither a thing, an object, nor simply a concept. God is a Person. As "persons," we must relate to a person, the Person. You as a person—heart, soul, mind, and strength—

must be attached to the absolute Person, who relates to your heart, soul, mind, and strength. Personal love for God shares similarities with the way persons lovingly relate to one another in daily life. What does it take to cultivate your love for a human being? Words, deeds, and gifts. Words, deeds, and gifts nurtured by an investment of your resources to show and cultivate love with any person correspond to how you must relate to the Person—God.

Why love *the* Lord God? Because God is the supreme Person. He should be loved simply because He is God. You are not to love Him as a means toward something else. You are not to love Him to get something out of Him, because what you get out of Him may usurp His place in your life as the Supreme Love.

Often repeated and varyingly interpreted in spiritual life literature, Bernard of Clairvaux delineated four kinds of loves: (1) "Love of self for self's sake." I call that non-Christianity. (2) "Love of God for self's sake." Carnal Christianity, isn't it? Instead, true spirituality is: (3) "Love of God for God's sake." That is mature Christianity. Bernard also added (4) "Loving self for God's sake"—to be experienced fully in heaven and only occasionally now.[1] The reason to love God is Himself.

Love God fully: With your entire being, your total life, with everything you are and have. Love Him with all that is you! In case you don't get the point, notice the four-time repetition of the phrase "with *all* your . . ." No part of you should love God less than other parts.

Love God wholly: You can't love Him with your head and not love Him with your heart and hands. Three great errors have marked Christian spirituality over the ages and are still with us. The first error I call the *headies*, the gnostics of the faith, the seminary types—the foolish people who don't transfer hearing to doing. Second, the *handies* are involved in service. They don't wait to hear but eagerly become God's hands for work. Then third, the *hearties* quiver with their livers, drip with emotion, and disengage their minds. I prefer falling into the second error than the first or the third. But they are all mistakes. No part of your life is spiritually prioritized or deemphasized in Jesus' foundational command.

Love God with everything you've got—with everything you are, know, and have. Loving Him is the only way to break the contest between your self-life and the God-life. Love is the way *of* obedience. It is the way *to* obedience. All we really wanted was His love, and everything came with it. He who spared not His own Son, how can He not with Him give us all things? (See Rom. 8:32.) All He wants is our love, for everything toward Him will be included in it from us.

You may be aware of the theoretical discussion in spirituality circles between the priority of "being" and "doing." Some hold that "to be is more important than to do." Yet others say "to do is more important than to be." At the gift shop of the Victoria Terminal of the Hong Kong harbor, I saw a resolution of that problem on an extra-large T-shirt:

Plato says: To be is to do.

Socrates says: To do is to be.

Frank Sinatra sings: "Do-Be; Do-Be; Do!"

Forget the academic discussion. If you have to love God as a whole person, it is "be-do." Or really "know-be-do," or better, "know-feel-be-do." You ought to know the one Lord you love; you ought to be a lover of God; and you ought to act on your love of God. With everything you've got—all you are, know, and have. Being in love with Him connects the hearing of His words to acting upon them.

Our love for God is a God-thing, but it is also God's thing. The impossible God-thing reveals God's expectations and my inability to meet those expectations. The inevitable God's thing provides His enablement for soil and foundation treatment. God doesn't make known His expectations without giving us His enablement—a distinctive feature of the Christian faith, a necessary feature of building the intentional life.

Explore with me some of the nuances of the four nouns that Jesus uses in the Great Commandment: heart, soul, mind, and strength. They carry identical weight and, strung together, reveal how comprehensive, connected, and cumulative the love of God ought to be. The repetition of near synonyms is not meant to specify acts or spheres of love. They were picked to intensify the absoluteness, exclusivity, and necessity of personal affection for God. They are coordinate, and concentric, and climactic in their parallelism. They well-integrate in you as a person, responding to the Person, in a personal way. I am going to look at each of the four phrases (nouns modified each time by "with all your") sequentially, in terms of the command, the problem, and the response, without overlooking the unity and overlap between them.

I. FIRST-LOVE: IS GOD THE PASSION OF YOUR HEART?

First-love is a God Thing! God's expectation of you is clear— a first-love relationship with Him. Hebrew anthropology saw the heart as the central organ of human life in all its dimensions—thought, conscience, temperament, body, and conduct. "The human heart, will, or spirit is the executive center of a human life. The heart is where decision and choices are made for the whole person."[2] Proverbs 4:23 reads, "Watch over your heart with all diligence, for from it flow the springs [all the issues] of life" (NASB, brackets mine). *Heart* can refer to the will, the volition, the gut-level love of something for which one will sacrifice anything. We reflect that meaning when we say, "I love you with all my heart."

An acquaintance of mine, not a very large guy, played quarterback for the Air Force Academy football team. He played with everything he had—overcoming obstacles, disadvantages, and debilities. Often we heard the following judgment about him, "The guy has got heart!" What did it mean? He went into the game wholesale, full-scale, no reservations, no holding back. In this Great Commandment, the whole person is in view with obedience beginning in the heart.

Jonathan Edwards, America's prolific, "original" theologian of the 1700s, emphasized the engagement of the heart as the seat of all religion.[3] "The nature of human beings is to be inactive unless influenced by some affection. Just as worldly affections are the spring of worldly actions, so the religious affections are the spring of religious actions." Your heart— the seat of personality, decisions, and values—commands your actions. Loving God from the heart is a heart moved by God, toward God.

Heart-love for God, then, describes that aspect of your relationship that commences in and with your personal center. Too often we reduce the Christian faith to a mixture of commands to obey, duties to observe, or laws to endure. Instead, the whole Christian life is but a lover's responsibility. God wants you to love Him, serve Him, trust Him, and fear Him, with all your *heart*. God does not want sterility or monotony in that relationship. He wants a relationship into which you put your heart.

Heart-love reveals first-love, priority love. What we love first, what we have set our hearts upon, settles the passion of life. So we've got to make our relationship to God top priority.

When it comes to first-love for God, it seems that life often schemes to keep God out of the heart, to edge Him out of central place. We face the problem of too many loves. Too many good things take over God's first-place position. Too many objects infiltrate the heart. Too many loyalties clamor for priority. Thus God is left out, downgraded, excused from daily existence. Instead of being first and last, He is at best the last among the first, or the first among the last. We live life without God in it—the secular or worldly life. We orient our lives around unfortunate, alternate questions—how best can I function or cope without God? How little can I include God in the substance and forms of daily life? Where can I get away from His influence?

If you don't think that you live by these realistic and tempting questions, here's a way to tell how influential God is in your life. Simply review the manner in which you have lived last month. Take out your to-do lists of tasks, schedules, and appointments. Where did God fit in them? Or look at your checkbook register for the last year. How eminently does God show up in the use of your monies? Heart-love for God is first-love, a priority relationship. Words, deeds, and gifts toward the Lord require resources of time, energy, and money that you would rather shower on your other loves.

In meeting God's expectation of love, we are presented with three options to address. In the existential dilemma of vibrant spirituality versus human deficiencies we must

(1) either reserve priority chunks of time, energy, and money for God;

(2) or let every expenditure of resource demonstrate the priority of God in our lives;

(3) or both options above.

Take work, for instance. The busyness of work easily demands first-love attention in terms of time usage. Ecclesiastes recommends, as I do, that we enjoy work. It's OK to welcome busyness. We complain about being busy but relish our complaint since the alternative is not enviable. How could we find a way of turning our work into demonstrating priority love for God? Here are a couple of hints. Apply the core values of the Beatitudes that you studied to your work situation—dependence on God, compassion toward others, perseverance in the middle of trials, and so on—thus sanctifying work as a means of exhibiting priority love for God. In those instances, work won't become an end in itself. It will act as a vigorous means of portraying first-love for God. Later we will consider our work life as part of our mission.

You could also face the problem of loving people too much. Now if we love people too much, we can't love God as first-love. But biblical commands exacerbate the issue by commanding us to love people. For instance, God says I must love my wife like Christ loved the church. Yet the Bible says we ought to love God as our first-love. How can a dual focus on seemingly absolute objects be maintained?

I recognize the biblical and existential tension and resolve it in the following manner. God clearly says we must love people. In fact, the second great command is to love your neighbor as you already love yourself. Apparently, God doesn't want us to feel the tension that we feel in the disjunction between loving Him and loving people. The Bible commands us to fervently love people (1 Pet. 2:17), but not to love the world nor the things of the world (1 John 2:15). Since God richly gives us all good things to enjoy (1 Tim. 6:17), you can enjoy your hobbies but not love them. You can enjoy your sports, but do not love them. You can enjoy your music, but don't love it. If your interests and hobbies are taking more of your energy, time, and resources than God does, then evaluate your heart for God—first-love.

But what about loving people too much? Can one love his wife and family too much? No, one can't love his wife too much, if the Bible commands you to love your wife as Christ loved the church. However, Jesus also says, "If anyone comes to me and does not hate his father and mother, his wife and children, his brothers and sisters—yes, even his own life—he cannot be my disciple" (Luke 14:26). Now how does one go about loving his wife as Christ loved the church and still be Christ's disciple? The apparent contradiction stands on Jesus' claim to be fulfilling the Old Testament in His teachings (Matt. 5:17). The Old Testament did say, "Love your neighbor" (Lev. 19:18). Indeed, Jesus commanded His disciples in the Sermon on the Mount to even "love your enemies"! Certainly He wouldn't *command* the love of enemies and hatred of parents! So, we must consider the matter more deeply.

"Hating" one's relatives in that difficult discipleship verse is not spoken or written in the *command* form. It follows a conditional, qualifying form. Jesus doesn't say "you must hate them"—with the command force that the Bible employs elsewhere for love of family and others. Therefore, "hating" takes a subordinate place to Jesus' explicit command to "love" neighbors and enemies. Yet there is a clarity to the hierarchy of objects of personal love. Your relatives shouldn't get in the way of your following Christ.

A man confessed that he had not made his wife number one in recent days, for golf had taken hold of him. As much as I appreciated his expressed commitment to his wife, I wanted him to make his wife number two in his life. Why? First-love is only reserved for God.

The last part of Jesus' hard saying goes: "even [hate] his own life." Obviously, one's own life can get in the way of a first-love relationship with Him. Your love for Jesus needs to come before your love for your family, even love for your own life. So you can't love your family too much, but you can love your family too much when compared to your love for God. If your family rather than God is your first-love, you are giving them God-status in your life. The one God must possess God-rank, first-rank status in your life. The love of God takes precedence over all other loves. That's why Jesus confirmed Simon by His post-resurrection questions: "Do you love me *more than these?*" He called for first-love from Simon.

Heart-love is priority love. Is your heart gift wrapped for God? If I were to ask your wife or your husband what consumes you, what would she or he say? If your children were asked about your main interests, what would they point to as your first-love attention? God wants you to seek His kingdom and righteousness *first* (Matt. 6:33). Your family makes the best witnesses to report how loving God first allows you to love them better!

Let me give you hope in the middle of first-love failure. You will prevail by God's enablement of your responses to Him. God's overtures in mercy and grace will woo you into giving Him first place in your life. He also takes responsibility to become number one in your life. He can do that legitimately, for He is the only nonarbitrary candidate for first-rank status. When I bestow or endow anything other than God with first-love, I fall into a subjective, relativistic mob of *first-loves.* God has no problem with many loves. He does insist on a point or two about too many first-loves. There is only one God!

Those who are married know that when their relationship with their spouse is healthy, everything else seems a little better, a little lighter. When the relationship is sour, a dark cloud seems to hover over other aspects of life. The marriage analogy should keep you from being afraid of making God your passion, for when you love Him firstly, you are able to love everything else rightly. When you don't, everything else suffers. That's why God commands a first-love relationship to Him, for it affects and energizes every other dimension of life.

Love Him for who He is with all your *heart,* with all you've got.

II. REAL-LOVE: IS GOD THE PASSION OF YOUR SOUL?

If heart-love points to first-love, soul-love expresses *real-love.* Jesus commands the love of God with all your soul. Soul-love communicates a God-thing as well.

Soul-love replicates the longing and loneliness associated with real-love. When was the last time you felt lonely for God? Not simply making intellectual statements of need, but really longing for Him, hungering and thirsting after righteousness (Matt. 5:6). *Psyche,* the Greek word for "soul," denoted the point of contact between the material and immaterial, the connection between the outside and inside, the link between the inner and outer person. Again, this word stands for the whole person in all one's faculties and facilities.

The Many Words for Love

Four words for love are used in Greek. Three of these Greek words dominate in the New Testament.

1. *Eros* stands for sensual, sexual love, reserved in the Bible for the love between husband and wife. A description of *eros* by kids arrived in my in-box:

   Mae (age 9): "No one is sure why it happens, but I heard it has something to do with how you smell. That's why perfume and deodorant are so popular."

   Glenn (age 7): "If falling in love is anything like learning how to spell, I don't want to do it. It takes too long."

   How do you make a person fall in love with you?

   Camille (age 9) says: "Shake your hips and hope for the best."

2. *Philos* stands for brotherly love. Friendship love that makes time, speaks truth, corrects errors, forgives faults, and goes on loving in common acts of friendship.

3. *Agape,* the term Jesus uses in the Great Commandment, names an unselfish, unconditional, unattached love. It seeks one's highest good on the basis of a decision of the will and an inclination of the heart. Jesus' command appears in the present active sense. We must keep on loving God.

So what does it mean to love God with all our soul? This invitation imperative—to love Him with all your heart and soul—includes an overlap of meaning. Since Hebrew psychology lacked precise terminology or, better, used wholistic terms, the Old Testament sometimes uses *heart* and *soul* interchangeably.[4]

Just like "heart," the biblical "soul" also includes one's volition—the fount of free decisions. We have to choose whom we will really love in life. When we mix *agape* and the volitional aspect of the soul, we are speaking of voluntary, purposeful love. Purpose to love the Lord your God under the direction of your will in self-giving, personal commitment.

Too often we confuse love with what precedes, accompanies, or succeeds it, whether goose bumps, laughter, or heartaches. Indeed, real-love is not an accidental, haphazard sensation. Love cannot be coerced, because a lover must decide to love the loved one. Neither is real-love merely consenting to what is already the case. God is already Lord, but you have to decide whether He will be important to you, in your heart and soul. When Jesus surreptitiously claimed deity status in the reinstatement of Peter (John 21:15–17) with the threefold repetition of "Do you love me?" He was asking that consensual question. Jesus basically asks, "Do you freely and really choose Me as your first and real-love, because by choosing Me you will create and acknowledge My increasing importance in your life until I really pull into first and foundational place among your allegiances?" Consider rereading that last sentence as an amplified version of Jesus' question to Peter for clearer contemplation. How do you answer Jesus' question?

Love and Emotion

The *soul* not only grounds one's actions, it is the source of emotions and desires. "Soul-love" must also be filled with that emotional aspect. In critical ways, your enthusiasm for a particular object reveals what you feel about it. And vice versa. Your emotion reveals what your heart and soul have selected as valuable to you.

I find Christians on both sides of the divide of emotional expression. Some eschew emotion in spiritual experience. Yet others are quite gullible, with emotions dictating spiritual vitality.

Numerous dangers lurk within a subjective reading of truth and reality. Subjectivism makes one's self the determiner of truth, one's experience the measure of reality, and one's psychology the arbiter of theology. To "follow your heart," to "discover your soul," to "obey your intuition" is to follow hazardous paths. In these senses and especially in the sense of religious irrationalism, "subjectivism" must be rejected. Irrational subjectivism can take immoral practices—group sex and drug overdoses—and declare them morally good, simply because they feel good. Even elevating values that are good in themselves (e.g., honesty) and loving them because they make us feel better is not quite the biblical love of God. Atheists, too, can be honest. Many Christians indulge in foundation maintenance—exercising good spiritual disciplines—merely to feel good or better about themselves.

Instead, loving Jesus with soul passion experiences God as someone important in *Himself,* meaningful in Himself, whether or not He performs for us. Non-Christians suspect that Christians follow Jesus for what we can get out of Him. The promise of health or wealth in Christian preaching reduces God from being important in Himself to being valuable because He can come through for us. I hasten to alert you: it is right to be involved with loving God, preoccupied with loving Jesus, simply because God is God. Soul passion after God, because He is good in Himself, is good in itself.

When the psalmist emotes about his desire for God, he confirms God's unequivocal significance in *Himself.* Psalm 42:1–2 reads, "As the deer pants for streams of water, so my soul pants for you, O God. My soul thirsts for God, for the living God. When can I go and meet with God?" Or, Psalm 63:1: "O God, you are my God, earnestly I seek you; my soul thirsts for you, my body longs for you." God is important in Himself. Objectively so. We need to be careful that loving God is not viewed as *right* because it is fun, or makes us happier, or gives us more peace.

However, emphasizing the emotions is not the necessary precursor to subjectivism in loving. Our hearts are depraved enough to prohibit our trust of emotions to interpret reality for us. We need to constantly evaluate motives and purposes in the light of Scripture to see that the Lord God is not just good because of His private benefit to us. Yet we must consider an issue within the objective value. Think about this statement: God is "important in Himself to me."[5] Many things are good in themselves, but there is a personal granting of special value to a specific object that is already valuable. Let me illustrate. My second son, Robby, and his dog show the granting of subjective importance to an objective value. All dogs are valuable, but Tugger (we lost Fudge some time ago) is valuable to Robby. He orients his life around "Tugs" and allows this "dumb dog" (Ryan, our first son's, devaluing of Tugger) to schedule his day, to claim his life.

So we have three options again, in the connection of objective and subjective value.

(1) *We can objectify a subjective value in choosing the right object to love.* For example, in moral errors— lying is turned into a value because it helps in difficult situations. When you seek to defend your lie by appealing to what people naturally do, for example in concealing sexual inappropriateness, you seek to objectify a subjective value. Others objectify morally

neutral tastes—endowing near-objective value on a product. Advertising does that with products, be it a Rolex, a BMW, or mint chocolate chip ice cream. When we positively succumb to advertising, we go after an image, persona, or concept to give value to us. But there is no *intrinsic* importance to those erroneous preferences. You just found out I prefer a certain ice cream flavor!

(2) *We can deny, decry, or devalue an objective good.* A dog is a good thing, but Ryan attaches no significance to Tugger. Honesty is good, but one devalues its intrinsic importance by being honest in order to feel better about one's self. Legalism in spirituality falls into this error. Going to church more often to feel better, especially better than your neighbor, is devaluing the good. God is an objective good, worthy of being loved for Himself, but we devalue Him by loving Him for self's sake.

(3) *We can choose an objective good for subjective value.* Robby does that with hugs for Tugs. The first commandment calls us to this posture in one's relationship with God. "In all loves, the value of the beloved is an 'importance in itself to me.' Without the 'to me' there would be no love in its subjective value. My life would not be bound up with the beloved. Without the 'importance in itself,' there would be no love in its objective good. Love is directed to the objective value of the beloved, a value that the beloved really or ideally has."[6]

So, loving God will also make you feel good or happy, but your experience of His goodness doesn't make Him a worthy object of love. The subjective consequence of an intrinsically valuable object—God, in this case—allows us to enjoy our relationship with Him. The psalmist, after longing for God's presence (important in Himself), goes on to the hope of emotively expressing praise in the temple for his own future deliverance (Psalms 42 and 43). In Psalm 63, the psalmist senses that God's love is better than life (v. 3). But his soul will be satisfied as with the richest of foods (v. 5), with singing lips (vv. 5, 7) and night remembrances of God (v. 6). His soul clings to God (v. 8) and will rejoice in God (v. 11). As expected, the answer between the will and emotion lies in between desire and duty. We need the solidity of duty and the fluidity of desire. We relish both obedience and wonder, joy and submission, desire and duty. Life's underlying *purpose* is loving God. The *result* of this soul passion is soul satisfaction. Unfortunately, we often confuse purpose and result. Take Christmas as an example—we think the purpose of Christmas is to give gifts, when gifts are simply the result of Christmas!

Remember the bumper sticker that read, "Do you really know Jesus?" I saw another one that asked, "Do you really love Jesus?" That question hit me at the level of subjective valuing of God, the supreme, objective treasure. Do I really cherish Him? Esteem Him? Enjoy Him, more than anything else in the world? Whether it is my son and his dog, or you and your computer, my neighbor and his car, my friend and his clothes, our choices for love smack of arbitrariness. Robby could have chosen another dog to love (and since has), or you could have chosen another computer with similar features to the one you currently own. When it comes to valuing God, however, He is the only nonarbitrary choice we will make. We can't choose another God, who is indeed God, with the same features and functions. We can't increase His importance in Himself, though we can intentionally increase His value to us.

We can also decrease His value to us—intentionally or unintentionally. Decreasing God's value to us exposes the nature of sin. If half-gods and demigods claim our first-love, sin, the anti-God penchant in us, siphons off our desire for God. Sin stifles joyful, soul-love for God. While sin begins in the immaterial, it evidences itself in the material. It expresses itself in the self-life. Ultimate love is arbitrarily given to arbitrary options, replacing real-love for God, the only nonarbitrary candidate. In the Bible, that choice is called and condemned as idolatry.

Consider the following questions as tools to help you identify places where God's value in your life is under attack:

> How does your love for Jesus exceed your love for sinning?

> Are you offended by anything at all, especially because it offends Him?

> To what degree do you feel estranged from Him when you sin?

> In what areas of your life would you be embarrassed if He were physically present with you? Are there acts of rebellion in your life that are not, in themselves, worth doing?

The realities of temptation continually challenge us as sin battles for our souls. Sin is always worse than it appears, even if we are not yet caught. Theologically speaking, cancer is better than sin. Losing your job is better than sin. Yes, death is better than sin. Sin is cosmic treason against the Holy God and we dabble with it as though it were of little significance. We are not yet convinced that sin is heinous in itself. Conversely, only loving Jesus is absolutely important in itself, because He is absolutely important in Himself.

If you really love Jesus, you should be able to answer a hard question: Are you willing to reach the point that you honestly have no desire to ever sin again? I trust you feel the burden of that question. I am not asking for perfection. That will not happen this side of heaven. I am asking if you are willing to have a longing to not sin again. Are you willing to say that sin must be completely crushed in you? Or are you disappointed that you might never get to sin again if indeed you make that decision? If that choice provokes disappointment, you can be sure that Jesus is not yet your real-love. If you really love Jesus in Himself, you will really hate sin in itself.

Which sin is easy for you? What sins don't bother your conscience any longer? Which sin is so enjoyable that you forget that it is sin? Which sins do you excuse with biblical, theological, and practical reasons? Sin, any sin, is sin against God, and thus *worse than* committing adultery in front of your spouse—certainly a grave sin. God wants your exclusive love. He wants to be your only soul-love and is jealous of anything that functions like God in your life. Real-love is often spontaneous and immediate. But it also can be planned and deliberate. Think about your love relationship with any human being. Spontaneous expressions blend with planned words, deeds, and gifts. Similarly, your love for God can be spontaneous and planned. In addition, your rejection of sin should be natural and premeditated.

Love Him with everything you are and everything you've got! *Soul*-love asks if you really love Jesus.

III. TRUE-LOVE: IS GOD THE PASSION OF YOUR MIND?

Your mind matters much in your love for God. This is unlike

many religions of the world, where one's mind doesn't matter at all. "Please remove your shoes and minds outside," insisted the sign in front of Oregon's Rajneeshpuram commune in the early 1980s. In sharp contrast, Jesus asks you to utilize your mind in loving God. The Old Testament assumed a wholistic notion of man and did not use the word "mind" even though it presumed it. So Jesus expanded Deuteronomy 6:5, or, better, explicated what the first command included. In Greek, "mind" is used with several prefixes for fine subtlety. The word Jesus uses here "focuses on one's ability to think or perceive and thus designates the mind with which one organizes perceptions."[7] The root word emphasizes the understanding, the intellect, the ability to reason abstractly, to reflect morally, and to desire rightly.

God's first commandment expectations include a knowledge aspect, even though you will never know God as God knows Himself. When we enter eternity, we will know ourselves as we are known (1 John 3:2), but God will remain greater than our vastly improved knowledge. We are going to be able to love God in eternity without omniscience; we can love Him now without the greater knowledge that heaven will provide.

The Great Commandment includes the mind, even though the natural mind is naïve. The mind thinks it claims independent status, to function as the Supreme Court of final adjudication, but those thoughts are extremely dependent on a web of prior beliefs.

Religious rationalism operates as deviously and insidiously as religious irrationalism. If sin affects and infects the entirety of our personal existence, we can't trust mind, or heart, or soul. Consequently, we need all of them to distrust each other, to balance each other, to keep us from errors, but most important, to submit to divine revelation. Our proneness to limitations and gullibility demands that the mind be renewed, reformatted, and restructured by spiritual regeneration. It is only then that loving the Lord with our minds allows the Lord to supervise, control, and instruct us in the right use of the mind in all areas of life.

We'll call "loving God with your mind" *true*-love. That phrase rhythmically fits with first-love, and real-love. True-love is not only loving God truly, and truly loving God, but loving truth as part of using our minds rightly in loving God. According to Scripture, both truth and error confront us, and it is possible to distinguish truth from falsehood. Otherwise, we will be doomed to loving the wrong object. We could rightly love a counterfeit object more than God.

In March 1997, the world stood aghast as thirty-nine people belonging to a cult ended their lives because they wanted to catch Comet Hale-Bopp on its way across the heavens. They dressed in loose clothing, packed a tote bag with travel clothes, and put on fancy sports shoes. They did not forget to take five dollars in their pockets. They believed in a loose mix of biblical religion and science fiction fantasies. If only they had loved God with their minds! If only they had read their Bibles well! If they had loved truth, they would not have been reckless.

Becoming True Lovers

How about you? Are God and His Word the passion of your mind? Since it takes the Bible to make us true lovers, how much of your Bible are you taking in? We have talked before about directly applying biblical truth. The wise man finds out what God says before he applies it. Are you reading your Bible regularly for that purpose? Biblical illiteracy among Christians has reached appalling levels. With access to dozens of versions of the English Bible, many still are not being educated by it. We read the newspaper first, and spend more time in front of a mirror brushing our teeth than studying the Scriptures. Devotional books become substitutes for the Scriptures. Christians are not reading their Bibles, and we ought to be ashamed of ourselves, for non-Christians sometimes know more about the Bible than you and I do.

In the Scriptures, God has given us *everything* necessary for life and godliness. Consider my italicized words in the following passage from the apostle Peter.

> Grace and peace be yours in abundance through the *knowledge* of God and of Jesus our Lord. His divine power has given us *everything* we need for *life* and *godliness* through our *knowledge* of him who called us by his own glory and goodness. Through these he has given us his very *great and precious promises,* so that through them you may *participate in the divine nature and escape the corruption* in the world caused by evil.desires." (2 Peter 1:2–4)

Peter finds the "knowledge of God" important enough to expand his words of greeting. False teachers claimed a knowledge of God. How would his readers understand the great and precious promises and distinguish true teachers from false teachers, except by using their minds under the Scriptures for differentiation? However, this right use of the mind cannot occur except through conversion—participating in the divine nature and escaping the world's corruption.

True-love for God calls for submitting our minds to Him as revealed in Scripture. The Bible is not God. In our attempt to keep the two distinct, we sometimes separate the two—wrongfully. A seminary alumnus bemoaned the fact that he had not grown spiritually while attending seminary: "Classes left me with a love for the Bible, but not for Jesus." I understand the intent of his statement, but a love for the Bible is part of one's love for God.

I find the two objects taking the same word for love in the psalms. On the one hand the psalmist says, "I love the LORD" (Ps. 116:1), and follows it up with, "Oh, how I love your law!" (Ps. 119:97; cf. vv. 113, 163, 165). We can look at verses where God and His Word are called "life," "light," "way," and "truth." To keep the law is to love the Lord (Josh. 22:5); and to love the Lord is to keep His commandments (Ex. 20:6; Deut. 5:10). John 14:15 says, "If you love me, you will obey what I command" (cf. John 15:10). A part of our self-knowledge of true-love for God arises from rightly relating to His Word.

I don't know what I would do without the Bible. The philosopher in me would create speculative theories, firmly planting my feet in thin air. The psychologist in me would dispense counsel with self-help and human-potential hypotheses. The politician in me would provide sociological and anthropological prescriptions without adequate and reasonable justification. I would be constantly confused and would in turn confuse others. Fortunately, I possess a Bible. So do you. God's Word is adequate for *all* of life and godliness.

George advised his son against premarital sex: "When I was growing up in the '40s, it was wrong to sleep with a girl before marriage. In the '60s it was OK to sleep with her, but it was wrong to get her pregnant. In the '80s all we are concerned about is not catching the disease!" Then he told me, "I wanted my son to understand that regardless of time or culture, the Bible transcends all generational preferences." God has spoken and has not stuttered, stammered, nor stumbled. God has spoken and has not overstated nor understated the case.

The love of God with our minds should not be debunked by postmodern penchants that call for skepticism about everything except itself. Our minds select what is right to believe, while our hearts select what counts as valuable. Jonathan Edwards "teaches us that the intellectual life and the passionate life should be friends, not enemies. Without the slightest contradiction it is possible to be both tough-minded and tenderhearted. What we learn to do is to descend with the mind into the heart and there wait in anticipation for the heavenly Whisper. We worship God with brain and viscera."[8] Scripturally, the intellectual life is a facet of the passionate life. Heart-love is not to be separated from or opposed to mind-love. The heart won't value, the soul won't price, what the mind can't or won't believe. Heart and soul may value what the mind doesn't know or believes wrongly. But they won't "respect" what the head rejects. God is the One the mind may believe, the heart may value, and the soul may treasure.

We get to link the mind to both pre- and post-passion examination. A God-oriented, biblically submissive mind will enable you to discard what should not be valued. It will instruct you in what is right and appropriate. Now, new insights may be gained by the mind because of a love relationship that is established and nurtured. For example, my love for my wife is not merely mental, but new "information" follows my commitment to her. I begin to appreciate her for the things I *didn't* know about her. I discovered her industry, discipline, and hygiene more so after my marital commitment. In the same way, by loving God with the mind after the initial embrace, we discover new dimensions of knowledge that we process in growing acknowledgment of

Him. As you journey in your love affair with Him, new information and insights emerge from the relationship.

Let me explain. God's input through His Word addresses a constitutional problem in my heart as deceitful and desperately wicked. Who can know the heart (Jer. 17:9)? I can exercise the gift of discernment on others, but I myself cannot know my heart as well as I should. I can't discern myself. I desperately need the Word of God to diagnose my stupidity, reveal my motives, and direct my decisions. We may add the role of spouse, kids, mentors, counselors, boards, accountability partners, and the church community to provide input on our moronism, but they too can be deceived. It is the Word of God that enables me to see the Man-in-the-X-ray, for I can interpret the Man-in-the-mirror through depraved mind-filters. The Word of God, however, is stubborn. The more I love God, the more I hear from Him, and the more I hear from Him, the more I see myself correctly, but also confidently. Very often you will look at Scripture and say to yourself, "I've never seen that before." I admit that even while writing this section I rejoiced in the scope of biblical enlightenment that I never appropriated or appreciated before, as my mind began to explore what I had not known before.

Love Him for who He is with all you've got. Including your *mind*. Chris "wants a child's heart, but a grown-up's head," said C. S. Lewis.[9] True-love points to the right object. It would be a shame to give true-love to false objects. True value, then, arises from and follows true-love.

IV. FULL-LOVE: IS GOD THE PASSION OF YOUR LIFE?

"Love God . . . with all your strength." Love God fully, wholly, without reservations, without conditions, with all your faculties of existence and being. Is this PASSION or what?

Our love for God follows an imperative and is not an option. Ponder our responsibility to love. We sometimes feel that when love is reduced to duty, it is no longer love. But be assured that when the effervescent edge of love dies, love doesn't die. One kind of manifestation of love may not be present, but that is not the absence of love. When we love God with all of our being, we look for love for Him in different places. Unless you are in active rebellion against God, intentionally disobeying His will, you can find love in your soul, heart, or mind. We cannot legislate the kind of evidence you must exhibit as external proof of your love for God. We could wonder about your love for Him, but we can't mandate a particular expression of love. We could even question the parity between internal and external Christian commitment, but we can't decree that love must be divulged in a specific format.

Rick, my friend, doesn't wear a wedding ring. I wear two! I am as bound to my wife as he is to his spouse. I wish he would wear a ring to publicly acknowledge his covenant. My double band shows my double-boundedness. "It is better to have one wife and two rings than . . ." I think it is wiser to wear a ring in public. However, I can't expect Rick to show his commitment to his wife in the same way that I do. And he needs to return the favor. In some ways, I could conclude that he loves his wife more than I do, even though he doesn't wear a ring. He cooks for her! When I play *chef de cuisine,* I create novel recipes that even our dog refuses to sample. Forms of love do not prove intensity of love. But there is a responsibility to love. If heart and soul includes volition, then sheer obligation, gut-based commitment, helps us to succeed in loving even when pleasant emotion is absent.

This is why I must reemphasize the meaning of passion

here. Biblically and historically, passion refers to the most excruciating time in Christ's life (cf. John 18–19).[10] When Jesus faces the cross, there is no lack of the Father's love. Christ's Passion follows His own declaration of being loved by the Father (cf. John 17:24–26). The duty of love, however, demands the Passion week. Neither the Father nor the Son exhibited frothy, gooey, frilly love in looking toward the Cross. Did They love each other less during the Passion? No. Did They love each other? Yes. Do not confuse the duty of love with the love of duty.

When the love of obligation overwhelms the obligation to love, a subtle shift occurs from the object of love to the loving itself. Many cults and cultures mistake the love of obligation to be the obligation of love. Obviously, the love of obligation is far better than the antinomian tendencies, at least for the preservation of culture. The "conservatives" in any culture extol the love of obligation. But the love of obligation can turn legalistic, becoming an end rather than a means in the process of loving, and thereby discarding the true object of love. The obligations of love flow from the object. The love of obligation flows from obligation itself. Contemporary culture deplores the "suffering" of love. Sentiment keeps "passion" from being defined in its lucid, volitional, obligatory dimensions. Sometimes it is sufficient to love regardless of the "feel." Feelings may or may not follow. But whatever feeling is, it is not a necessary component of passion.

Remember the passive aspect of passion? The popular notion of passion is related to that which we *actively* pursue. Even if passion doesn't refer to suffering in present use, it includes a passive aspect. In passionate loving, the beloved object "acts upon" the lover and thus influences and even changes him. Therein lies the connection between "suffering," "emotion," and the human "passive." When a person "suffers," he is controlled, possessed, directed by some emotion. Presumably this addition of meaning is how the word *passion* came to refer to the emotion alone.[11]

Passion could be morally neutral—"his passion is auto racing"; or biblically directed—"you shall love the Lord your God with everything you've got, whatever it costs." Choose to passionately love that which will change you in the right way, for you will *passively* yield to the object of your love. In passion, you declare your willingness to be changed by the object. In some way you are making a decision about yourself, for yourself, in choosing the appropriate object. Ask yourself what object deserves the rights of your passion, your suffering, your reception. Passion is active reception and receptive action. What or who deserves that kind of love? Be very careful with your answer. We won't doubt the vitality of your passion, but we will question the legitimacy of its object.

Full-strength love of God denotes valid passion. It includes emotion. It may be negative emotion, and not the visible, visceral kind. Or it could be the loud, external expression of emotion. It really doesn't matter. There is never a time when a person is not emotional. He or she may not be emotional on the outside or "emotional" as defined by culture. Still, the most staid, analytical, cool mind emotes in its own ways. Read the book of Psalms for the full range of strong emotional passion toward God—positive and negative, intense and easy, loud and soft, external and internal. If you are filled with wonder, love, and praise, you find resonance in the praise and thanksgiving psalms. Crying for help and can't wait for God's intervention? Read the lament psalms. Would you like to express trust toward God? Do you need to repent before God? Do you need to reveal your anguished distress? Stay in the Psalms. You'll find strong emotion (informed by good theology) in the widest variety of circumstances.

Your full-love love-life, then, affects every aspect of life. The literal meaning of *affect* is to "act upon" (Latin *ad*, "to," "upon"; *facio*, "to do"; cf. mentioned in our discussions of Passion earlier). Consequently, you are not only acted upon (the passive aspect of passion), but you also act upon (strongly pursue) what acts upon you. You "endeavor after, desire, court"[12] that which affects every aspect of life. You know how it is when you are in love. Waking hours, sleeping hours, eating hours (do you eat for hours each day?), working hours, are affected by your passion. Your love-life affects every aspect of life. It is no wonder that God calls you to love Him with every aspect of your life.

If affection is that which you court, pursue, and endeavor after, then it denotes the object that draws your zeal. As said before, the critical link between ambition for the loved object and your action is "affection." When Paul challenges us to keep seeking and to set our *minds* on things above (Col. 3:2), he understands the role of affections in all areas. In fact, the King James Version translates Colossians 3:2 as, "Set your affection on things above."

Full-love for God, with all our strength, captures the climactic, connecting, comprehensive term to conclude the Great Commandment. Full-strength love catches it all—will, mind, and emotion—and concentrates them on the only worthy object of passion: the Lord your God. Unless the God-thing is settled decisively and soon, don't worry about the rest of your life in its worth, accomplishment, or length. A word that Edward Vacek coins affirms the truth, "The history of

Christianity is often told in terms of *orthodoxy,* the truth of doctrines believed; and Christians are frequently evaluated in terms of their *orthopraxy,* the good they do. But the inner history of Christianity is what we might call its *orthokardia,* the ordered affections that unite us with God, ourselves, other people and the world."[13]

Notice also that Jesus' great imperative is found in the future active form: "You shall keep on loving the Lord God, from the present to the future." Our passionate love for Christ must be ongoing from now on. We don't want to experience love-blockage or yield to a love-stoppage. Any time we sense the diminution of the love of God, we must turn that self-knowledge into spiritual focus toward Him. Not writing in my journal for a few days throws me off balance. I don't see this habit as a legalistic, merit-mongering exercise at all. Some basic disciplines are simply routines, checks, and necessities in a full-function life. If I don't brush my teeth for half a day, I can tell I need to. For a whole day, and my wife, with exaggerated olfactory sensitivity, can tell I need to. For two days, everyone else knows what I have missed. Similarly, missing my regular time with God alerts me to my need to jump-start my friendship again. In fact, I have to use times of spiritual fatigue as prompters to get back into our love relationship again. In His command, God doesn't envision a time when I wouldn't be in love with Him as a natural necessity. Only the cares and pleasures of this world choke my interests in Him. I must continue carrying on with Him, even as He continues carrying me and carrying on with me. Into the future.

"You shall" calls for a personal, individual response. Everything in this chapter, book, and series presumes your underlying, personal passion. While Christianity is personal, our passionate love is not private. Mystics may make that mistake. Engrossed in existential participation with the beloved, reflection becomes self-absorbed spirituality and turns into navel-gazing. They want to replicate past experiences with God and then get frustrated with Him for not showing up as He did earlier. Or, they want to duplicate someone else's experience in their own lives and then wonder if they have met the conditions for the extraordinary experience. Too many Christians are disappointed and get away with less than full-love for God because they see Christianity as a private enterprise. As a result, we've got decaffeinated Christians living in a decaffeinated Christian culture exhibiting decaffeinated Christian commitment.

Instead, biblical passion does not permit passion for private consumption. One of the reasons Jesus adds the second commandment as a core commandment is to prevent the self-oriented life. Without taking as much as a breath, the Lord goes on to "love your neighbor as yourself." Notice the second command is not only attached to the first, but "the second is *like* it" (Matt. 22:39, italics mine). Loving God is an individual response to God in the context of neighborly love. A part of your first, real, true, full love for God is demonstrated in the middle of the human situation. If you can't love your neighbor whom you can see, how can you love God whom you can't see (cf. 1 John 4:20)?

So, full-strength love arises in the context of a commitment to neighbor. George Macdonald remarked, "The love of our neighbor is the only door out of the dungeon of self."[14] As we journey into the Mission and Vision aspects of the Intentional Life, I want you to keep your roots grounded in and founded on your Passion. Loving your neighbor without loving Christ is as false as loving Christ without loving your neighbor. Later you will interact with serving Christ's ultimate purpose in personal calling as the unique way to loving your neighbor. God has prepared good works in eternity for us to fulfill—in terms of our neighbor.[15] A life of love toward God shapes a life of love toward neighbor. Your intentional life begins in the interior, but doesn't end there. It controls, frames, and results in an effective exterior life, and you will get to know the God you love better. You will also get to love the Lord you know better. We'll later see that our mission and vision explores the meaning and evidences the significance of our love for God.

TRANSFORMING LOVE

Now comes the practical question: *How can we love someone we haven't seen, and yet love Him constantly?* Mind-love helps with this question. God can preoccupy your mind even when you are not consciously thinking of Him. One vacation morning I decided to put air in our van's tires since they all seemed a bit low. While filling them up, I discovered a nail lodged in my left front tire. It was early morning in the middle of a small town, nine miles south of Nowhere, Nebraska, and I couldn't get the tire repaired. Since the tire wasn't losing air I decided to drive to the next town, only to find it a couple of hundred miles away. At first I kept thinking of the nail in the tire, watching for signs and effects of deflation. Soon car conversations turned to story audio tapes, laughter, and "he's touching me!" complaints from the kids. But the nail in the tire lingered in the crevices of my mind. The issue sat there, resurfaced to consciousness every so often, and then recessed as the next thing took over our thoughts and time. The nail preoccupied my mind when I was not thinking of it, not unlike your first, real, true, and full love for God.

Yesterday someone asked me if I think in English. Raised

bilingually, I revert to my mother tongue during times of senti-ment to express endearment, but I think I think in English. It's simply there. Another example: "A child's awareness is so absorbed in his mother that although he is not consciously thinking of her, when a problem arises, the abiding relationship is that with the mother."[16] Your love of God can be simply there, affecting every aspect of life, like the nail in the tire, the language in which you think, and a child and its mother. As long as we don't equate cognition with feeling, our mind can operate with background awareness of God even though we are not thinking of God. The phenomenon happens among lovers, especially engaged couples awaiting their wedding day. Immersed in love, they fully go about life. The song in their hearts, the lightness of their steps, the lilt in their souls, the smiles on their faces, all give away the fact, even the object their of love. We do not have to be thinking of things to know them, to be conscious of love to love. Love can be easily seen when our consciousness is fully directed to them; but to be fully directed *by* them, even though at any given time it may not be directed to them, gives away the fact and object of our love.

Loving the Lord God is the best choice you can make with-out arbitrarily endowing value on less than ultimate objects. As you love Him you come to appreciate His qualities more fully. Since you have chosen to make Him most important to you, you will find that He becomes more than most important. He becomes your very life, without becoming you. He becomes the source, the significance, and the shaper of your life. He wants us to freely choose Him, for as we keep on choosing Him, our choices will create His further importance in our life.

In the final sense, loving God is *responsiveness* rather than responsibility. You may feel extremely burdened as you reflect on your shortcomings in terms of God's expectations. Almost certainly we allow competing passions, conflicting values, and confusing objectives to take the singular place of God. I have encouragement for you in your onward pursuit of Christ as your passion. The God-thing is really God's thing.

You live under the enablement of God in loving God. In John 17:17, Jesus prays that God would "sanctify"—or "holy-fy"—His disciples in the truth. First Thessalonians 5:23–24 reads: "Now may the God of peace Himself sanctify you entirely; and may your spirit and soul and body be preserved complete, without blame at the coming of our Lord Jesus Christ. Faithful is He who calls you, and He also will bring it to pass" (NASB). God is the One who "sanctifies" (Heb. 2:11, NASB). May "he work in us what is pleasing to him" (Heb. 13:21).

It is just like God to maintain ways to work Himself into first-love place in your life. Since the all-powerful, fully good God covets primordial status in your life, He is able to secretly, surreptitiously, and stealthily turn you into a willing lover, to love Him more than anything else in the world. Remember the romance phenomenon. Did my wife turn me into her lover? Yes, but freely. In fact, I can't tell anymore whether I chose her or if she chose me, though she makes me think that I chose her. Theologically, God chose you; but you think you chose Him!

Let me explain how God's final, first-place victory happens in your life. When you became a Christian, you entered a new and different sphere of existence. You became a new creation. You left the sphere of death to enter life. You left Adam to belong to Christ. You left the realm of the law and came into the province of grace. You entered a new world, a new environment, a new culture. Your entry was real. The new creation was genuine. Consequently, the new newness is going to inevitably prevail. You shall not be the person you used to be, thinking the things you used to think, doing the things you used to do, because you were transferred from death to life.

That's just like when I first came to the United States. A brand new culture totally enveloped me. My adjustment was quite the cross-cultural experience. Everything was different—the food, the language, the customs. I remember going into a McDonald's and asking for a hamburjer, and was told, "Sir, it's not a hamburjer. It's a hamburger." I replied, "I'm sorry, I'm a stran-g-er here." And those wonderful black-and-white portraits in the post office. I asked the postmaster about them. He said, "Those are the FBI's most wanted criminals." I asked why the FBI didn't keep them when they had a chance to take the pictures! I parked once under a sign which said "FINE FOR PARKING," and was accused of violating traffic laws. But the new culture has begun to dominate me so that people in my birth-land think I think like those in my adoptive-land, let alone dress and speak like one. But don't ask native-born Americans, who think I have a long way yet to go before that is true.

Yet I have truly entered a new sphere. I left Asia at a point in time. I entered the U.S. at a point in time. My stamped passport proves I am in the U.S. But in many ways I still behave as if I was in the old culture, because of my long-term subservience to it. Some habits are quickly changed, yet others have been in me for a long, long time. They, too, will be changed.

A week into my new environment, I started adjusting to changed eating, sleeping, and driving patterns. Since I now lived in a new culture, I had to live in its ways. There are some habits about me that will take a long time to change because they are so ingrained in me—pronunciation of certain words. However, I am slowly being transformed into the priorities, patterns, and practices of the new culture. Actually, the change is not automatic. I occasionally relapse. But change is inevitable. If I rebel against the new culture, the change is slower—check the many immigrant conclaves in the U.S. Yet as I am open to the new hybrid-culture, change is more rapid. I could always retreat to my Indian-ness, speak my provincial language, and associate with others from my old territory. But when I am with the dominant culture, I speak to be understood. I have been affected and am being changed.

In the same way, loving the Lord Jesus will eventually win. Your love for God as primary love presently competes with several other loves. You should expect it. You used to love those alternates a whole lot. However, you have really entered a new sphere of spiritual existence. While you still carry some past baggage, God slowly transforms you to reserve and give first, real, true, full-love for Him. Occasionally you retreat into former life-patterns in consonance with old habits and values. But you have been affected and are being changed by this new dominant environment. The new culture will prevail even during extended times of rebellion. And however much you want to, you can't re-create the old country, though you may behave like you were there. If any person is in Christ, he or she is a new creation, the old has gone, the new has come! (cf. 2 Cor. 5:17). The new environment will win.

Put foundation and passion together, and you can see how life stabilizes by foundational commitments and grows by passionate focus. With the right soul passion as your sole passion, your life has something to stand and build upon. As the foundation is maintained, passion stirs. When passion is stirred, the entire life-structure benefits with strength and affects the surrounding environment.

"Love Him for who He is with all you've got" represents a slogan restatement of the first commandment. When we get entangled with many first-loves, distracted by other lovers, directed to alien values, God calls us back to loving Him first. After all, we love Him because He first loved us. He loved us with all He's got. Our response is to love Him with all we've got.

Back to Fudge, our lonely, easily distracted dog and absolute proof of the relativity of beauty. Fudge began to dig his way out of our backyard to run away. Usually he came back within the evening. One time he didn't return. Robby, our dog-doting son, called out for him, "Fudge, Fudge," at the height of his preteen-aged shrill voice. "Come back, come back!" Fudge didn't. The next morning, Robby left the kennel door and the back gate open. Fudge didn't come back. Rob put out food in the dish, water in the pan. One day turned into days. Barely awake, Robby dashed out each morning to see if Fudge had returned. He would go to school, preoccupied with the loss of his dog. After school, he would rush into the house, fling his backpack on the sofa, and run to see if Fudge had come back. Fudge wasn't there. He served more fresh water and fresh food. The gate was still open. Later that week, we went to the animal protection shelter (a euphemism for "city pound"). Fudge was there. Boy and dog jumped with joy upon reuniting.

Perhaps your first-love priority for Christ has waned over the years. You've simply run away. He yells for you to "come back." The banquet is set, the water is ready, available for you to quench your thirst and satisfy your hunger. Just come on back. God loves you more than Robby loved his dog. He loves you with heart, soul, mind, and strength. Having known all there is to know about you, He still loved you, chose you, saved you, and now awaits your return to His first-love.

Nothing can take His love away from you, but many things can take your love away from God. Will you make Him your first, only, true, and last love? Come on back to loving Him. Although you've run away many times, He'll take you back. Love Him for all He is—the One Lord, your God. Love Him with all you are, feel, know, and with all you have. God's thing is to transform your life into the God-thing, so that your sole passion will be God Himself.

What is our personal response in maintaining passion as the foremost component of an intentional life? A strong life-structure cannot be built on a weakening foundation. We turn now to some practical steps in maintaining the foundation on which life is built.

Nurturing Passion

Foundation-repair in our North Texas home was completed at the end of a forgettable—really an unforgettable—summer. Our bank account suffered severe weakening, but the foundation of our house was rein-

forced. Cracks closed, doors shut quietly, closets opened less stubbornly. Within a year, however, my wife began observing cracks in the wall again. My fine-tuned male powers of sensory perception took a little longer to notice the obvious.

Initially we only protested internally—cracks shouldn't appear after we spent so much money. Was the extra high expense (add emotional costs to the dollar layout) worth the effort? We looked up the ten-year-warranty from the foundation repair company. You guessed it. New cracks were not covered by the "comprehensive" warranty! The experts came out, looked at the fresh fissures, pronounced the foundation in good shape, and identified a new explanation for the problem. We needed to maintain the foundation by keeping the moisture of the external soil constant. They suggested that we run water through porous hose placed all around the foundation of the house.

Why? Summer heat and drought hardens North Texas "gumbo" clay soil. That hardening alters the friction between the bearing piles and soil, causing the foundation to shift. In order to protect a newly repaired foundation, the soil around the house must be kept moistened. In our region, foundations demand year-round, lifelong attention.

The "necessary thing"—your salvation—on the "bedrock"—Christ Jesus—cannot be moved. He is the un-rockable, unshakable, unflappable foundation of your salvation. One theological reason for your salvation's permanent security arises from the quality of your bedrock. Christ secures your salvation for you forever. Once you receive eternal life, through the crisis of transferring your trust to Him alone, you receive *eternal* life. If eternal life could be lost, it wouldn't be *eternal*. Your salvation issue is settled.[1]

However, you can lay a poor foundation on that bedrock. Laying the right foundation comes from embracing Jesus—hearing and doing His words. Reinforcing the foundation provides staying power through the vicissitudes and vacillations of life. When we neglect or reject Christ's authority over our lives, we nullify the strength of our spiritual foundation by introducing foolishness into wisdom, sin into godliness, transgression into holiness. Christ's expectations of us are neither heard nor kept. The foundation itself doesn't break, but our anchoring pillars can shift. Interior cracks will appear. Therefore, we must maintain the foundation by soil moistening. Foundation maintenance is an integral part of house upkeep.

I liken "soil moistening" to nurturing a vital, spiritual life—nurturing our passion. I especially connect soil moistening to watering our lives by means of spiritual disciplines—providing an environment for the new life to flourish.[2] If we don't apply the moisture of the spiritual disciplines into our lives, uniformly, year-round, and lifelong, we'll generate severe structural damage. The foundation will shift. We will be ignoring and disobeying what we hear to be God's Word. We will become carnal Christians; Christian fools, making the oxymoron a tragic, verifiable reality. We will become Christian in name only, like the "ONE HOUR DRY CLEANERS" who turned away my friend in urgent need for laundry service with, "That's not what we do. That's only our name!"

SPIRITUAL DISCIPLINES FOR FOUNDATION MAINTENANCE

Here is a quick summary of the spiritual disciplines for foundation maintenance, for moistening the soil around our lives. Spiritual disciplines were never meant to be confined to seminaries, or, forgive the comparison, cemeteries. They offer an indispensable part of each person's spiritual upkeep, to hear and obey God's Word. They integrally relate to the ongoing authority given to Jesus, the rock foundation. The spiritual disciplines water our foundation.

The Bible straightforwardly refers to spiritual discipline. First Timothy 4:7 states, "Train yourself to be godly" (NIV), or, "Discipline yourself for the purpose of godliness" (NASB). Louw and Nida define the Greek word *gumnazo*, "To experience vigorous training and control, with the implication of increased physical and/or moral strength—'to train, to undergo discipline.' . . . 'to control oneself by thorough discipline'—'to discipline oneself, to keep oneself disciplined.' In a number of languages the equivalent of 'to discipline oneself' is literally 'to make oneself obey.' This may some-times be expressed idiomatically as 'to command one's heart.' It is the training of the body or the mind, physical and mental sensibilities (cf. Heb. 5:14)."[3] The Bible views spiritual disciplines as compatible with the spiritual life and comparable to physical fitness programs. It is the commanding of the heart toward godliness.

Healthy practice of the spiritual disciplines avoids both legalistic and manipulative approaches. We fall into salvific error if we seek God's favor by means of the disciplines. They are neither meritorious nor sacramental in the saving sense. Spiritual disciplines are neither the basis nor the source of spiritual growth. They are not the means to faith, nor do they empower it. Instead, they are our overflow response to God's expectations and provisions. They are the means that God uses to produce godliness in you and me.

In the Old Testament, two basic covenant terms were "love" and "faithfulness." There is no love without faithfulness and vice versa. Spiritual disciplines reveal the faithfulness of love and are not meant to demonstrate the love of faithfulness.

View the spiritual disciplines not so much as skills to develop but as habits to implement. Disciplines are not like playing the piano when you hate it. They are more like brushing your teeth because you need to. God does not ask you to get better at the disciplines, though that is a result. While there are better and worse ways of brushing your teeth, you don't need to develop increasing skills in brushing your teeth. You just need to do it. Similarly, you may practice the disciplines well or poorly, but you can't develop them too much beyond the essentials. You can pray adequately or inadequately, but you cannot develop skills too much beyond the basics in praying. Once you view disciplines as skills, you live within a hairbreadth of legalism. If you become stronger at the discipline than in your relationship with God, your concern for discipline may wrongfully displace your concern for God Himself. It is possible to start pursuing your own goals for holiness over those of intimacy with God.

Spiritual disciplines cannot hasten spiritual growth, but growth can be delayed by lack of or error in spiritual disciplines. God doesn't give us long-lasting teeth. He gives us long-lasting teeth as we brush. God doesn't give us the godly life. He gives us the godly life as we are godly.

Don't worship the habit, but you can't worship God without the habit. You've got to practice them without realizing it, until they become second, almost instinctive nature. "The right thing to do with godly habits is to immerse them in the life of the Lord until they become such a spontaneous expression of our lives that we are no longer aware of them."[4] The spiritual life is intentional and informal. Like any solid and growing friendship,[5] it is maintained intentionally.

COMMON INGREDIENTS

Common ingredients of effective disciplines include practice, context, and direction.

Practice, as intimated in the previous paragraph, is just doing it—pursuing godliness and obeying Scripture. While we may develop skills, we don't want the skills to supplant the practice of what we know already must be done. You can get better at studying the Bible as a skill, but that should not keep you from studying the Bible as a habit. We don't want to confuse *understanding* the practice of biblical giving with *undertaking* the practice of biblical giving.

The context for spiritual disciplines arises from life

circumstances. There will be certain times when you abandon yourself to specific disciplines. When you need divine direction, there is no substitute for intense focus on the Lord and His Word, mixing reflection, prayer, and consultation with the Christian community to keep the soil around your foundation the right consistency.

Direction in the disciplines may come from spiritual leaders. Leaders throughout church history possessed knowledge, experience, and strategies for the spiritual life. Today, God has given us pastors, teachers, mentors, and authors who help us apply godliness. Spiritual leaders, past and present, insist that spiritual disciplines form the foundation for spiritual vitality, bridge our hearing and doing, and fashion the soul.

I have seen various lists of biblical disciplines—from a dozen to twenty[6]—but place all of them into four kindred groups: alignment, attachment, detachment, and engagement. These groups are helpful for classification and are entirely connected.[7] My last group specifically deals with discovering and nurturing the Intentional Life, but all of them are necessary for an ongoing moistening process in maintaining the foundation, in keeping the soul supple.

1. Disciplines of Alignment

Disciplines of *alignment* have to do almost completely with familiarity and obedience to Scripture. Reading, hearing, meditating, studying, and memorizing Scripture put into practice the psalmist's obsession with God's Word. Hearing and doing Scripture is the mother of all disciplines because Scripture is our mother. We learn about the other disciplines from Scripture. Intimacy with God is more than the printed text of Scripture but cannot be outside or contradictory to it. We build on its borders and align to its boundaries. The Bible is good for doctrine, reproof, instruction, *and* training in righteousness (2 Tim. 3:16). Invite the Holy Spirit of heaven to remind, encourage, and facilitate alignment to God's expectations and direction. Alignment disciplines focus on the illumination of life, so that experience doesn't become the final determiner of God's truth, the arbiter of God's realities, or the maker of life's policies.

The Bible's ability to address the human condition astonishes the maturing person. Though I don't remember the precise instance, I recall moping after some comment my wife made. I believe she violated gender, cultural, and national pride! Unable to be man enough to initiate the reconciliation process, I turned to my morning devotional reading. It just "happened" that God's clarity in Ephesians 5 clobbered me with "love your wives, just as Christ loved the church." I had to choose to align with divine authority, clarity, and truth at that time. When I obeyed, my adamant soul softened, and my spiritual life brightened.

2. Disciplines of Attachment

Spiritual disciplines of *attachment* include positive actions that orientate us to the love of God. Personal communication—worship, thanks, and supplication—attaches us to the Lord and require time. Worship—personal and corporate—brings us near the person of God, who comes near as we draw near to him (James 4:8). Thanksgiving as a daily discipline (instead of being nationally reserved for a festive football and food-focused day once a year) overwhelms us with the goodness of God. Reflections on God's creation fill our senses with wonder, humility, praise, and love. Increasing appropriation of Jesus' amazing salvation work on the cross fixes and affixes our hearts on Him. If life is at cross-purposes, attach yourself to the purpose of the cross. Attachment disciplines focus on the illumination of the heart. They enhance our friendship with God.

One of the finest gifts I ever received was an empty composition notebook with my name and "prayer journal" printed on it. For me, the first act of reflective writing each workday turns into love toward God. Another friend presented me with a "Worship" Bible. As I said before, my spiritual life becomes disheveled if I go for a few days without writing in that journal or reading my Bible. My foundation shifts less easily when spiritual soil maintains moisture.

3. Disciplines of Detachment

Disciplines of *detachment* draw us away from the world, the flesh, and Satan. Disciplines of silence, solitude, and sacrifice give us new reserves against spiritual enemies. Intentional deprivation from pleasure—food, sex, shopping, entertainment, whatever—balances pursuits, centers perspective, and reinforces right priorities. We are called to be separated from worldliness. Suffering, in Christian discipline, does not carry romantic overtones as in some religious systems. We don't look for suffering; neither do we run from it. Suffering can break up idolatrous crutches in our lives and prepare the ground for training in godliness. Confession of sin, a specific biblical condition for cleansing, allows a range of spiritual dynamics to invigorate and moisturize life.

4. Disciplines of Engagement

Disciplines of *engagement* point to what foundation experts tell us—that *excessive* water and improper drainage can also create foundation problems. Positive drainage includes diverting runoff water away from the foundation. Excessive water in spiritual upkeep compares to attachment, detachment, and alignment disciplines without engagement. The spiritual disciplines of *engagement,* in serving people, disallow a purely privatized view of the spiritual disciplines. If the disciplines of detachment break our tendency to be too much *of* the world, the disciplines of engagement guide our practice of living *in* the world.

Our world contexts expand from nuclear and extended families, to church and society, both locally and globally. Our life-specific mission builds on a spiritual life foundation, and depends on the spiritual life for ongoing vibrancy. The engagement disciplines encourage the discernment of God's will for a person's life, to find out where God is calling for personal involvement, to track the times and the trends in order to fulfill one's life for God. Oswald Chambers writes: "It is easier to serve or work for God without a vision and without a call, because then you are not bothered by what He requires."[8] How can one discover personal vision, define calling, and identify giftedness to fulfill God's purpose for one's life? The latter books of the Intentional Life trilogy will address that question.

Soil moistening, then, must affect the following parallel dimensions:

> Cognitive, affective, behavioral

> Knowing, feeling, doing

> Head, heart, hands

> Doctrines, dynamics, disciplines

Nourishing our relationship with God, moistening the hardened soil around our hearts, keeping spiritual temperature stable—all describe a vibrant spiritual life. The habits involved prevent structural damage from soil shifts that our old nature, our environment, and our enemy orchestrate to move us off the Rock Foundation.

Biblical spirituality rejects the generic, mindless, content-less pursuit promoted by numerous religious groups that increasingly compete for your attention. You can access Thich Nhat Hanh's web site to lead you in spiritual meditation. There, you click on the "Mindfulness Bell" to remind you that we live in a spiritual universe. Or you take off your shoes (you *must* physically take off your shoes) to benefit from "the world's first interactive multimedia yoga instruction web site" at www.yogaclass.com. Digital spirituality allows many spiritual communities to serve everywhere, all the time, but their pervasiveness has little to do with the truth. Those teaching on Real Audio possess no divine powers. In the early days of Internet prowess, a grandmother used to take off her shoes as soon as she asked her grandson to fire up the computer to access her favorite spirituality site. She believed that the person inside the computer could see her just as she could see him, and wanted to appear barefoot for the full benefits of enlightenment.

The reason we highlight the foundation of Jesus is to emphasize the theological substructure, the unique biblical content, and the entire worldview framework for Christian spirituality in any life.[9] A vital, valid, vibrant biblical spirituality is built on the foundation of Jesus regardless of the variety of human circumstances, and thrives by the framework of that foundation. *Biblical* spirituality is the bridge between knowledge and action, hearing and obedience, in any life and each circumstance—the means of embracing Jesus' words and works into one's life.

I commend to you this view of spirituality as the foundational component of living an intentional life. Jesus-centered spirituality is foundational in two senses:

> ➤ Foundational in terms of *chronology*. You don't want to build foundations after you build the building.

> ➤ Foundational in terms of *ontology*. Your life must derive ongoing strength from a spiritual foundation. Spiritual vitality precedes and undergirds an effective, intentional life. Once it is filled with the content of Jesus, it becomes truly Christian.

Randomness and ineffectiveness (in addition to patterns of personal sin) characterize the lives of carnal Christians. They exhibit severe structural damage, because they have moved off the foundation. They heard Jesus' words but did not continue to do them. Instead, anti-Christian elements in thought and environment have made shambles of their lives. The soil around their salvation foundation became hard. The sub-structure of their lives shifted.

Carnal Christianity has turned into the curse of Christianity. Multitudes of senile spiritual babies, happy with a secure foundation, yet with no real structure to show, surround us like vast unfinished subdivisions. Their chaotic life-construction sites show little progress and already display cracks and fissures in foundation walls. Carnality leads to Unintentional Christianity. Unbelievers sense no attraction to the Way, the Truth, and the Life, because Christians live random, sin-filled, ineffective lives.

Instead, maturing Christians intentionally keep the soil moist by watering their spiritual lives. They see Jesus as both the chronological and ontological foundation of their lives. They pursue a spirituality formed by the Holy Spirit, informed by the Bible, and in conformity to the Lord Jesus Christ. One cannot live the Intentional Life as designed by

God without a spiritual relationship to him. Christian spirituality forms the basis for the rest of life's enterprise. Whatever else we are and do, we must begin with the Lord Christ as life's foundation, and reinforce the spiritual foundation as our sustaining strength.

EXPOSING OUR FOUNDATION TO CHANGE

Meanwhile back in North Texas, we were plagued by continued problems with structural cracks. We discovered that several foundation repair systems on the market offered us serious alternatives for repairing our home. Each system comes with its own advantages and disadvantages. Concrete pads provide quick, cheap, temporary fixes. Bell Bottom Pier repair furnishes a permanent solution when properly installed. A Simple Pressed Piling method drives pilings made of pre-cured/stressed concrete deep into the soil to enable leveling of the structure.

The chief drawback of each of these systems involves the lack of reinforcement to prevent the shifting of the pads, piers, or pilings. Hence a company in North Texas, Olshan Foundations, invented their Cable Lock System (U.S. Patent No. 5,288,175) that challenges the others by including anti-shift controls. The entire pile system is locked together with tensile cables (200,000 p.s.i.) enabling the substructure to act as an anchor to prevent upheaval during freeze-thaw cycles.

I wish I had heard about this company before we expended emotion, energy, and equity. It's too late for our house, but not too late for our lives. Salvation is like the cable-anchor that Olshan's technicians press into the ground at predetermined locations. Our salvation plays an active role in aligning the foundation that we lay on the Rock—Jesus. That cable runs through the center of each concrete piling and is locked into place by a piling cap.

May I equate the piling cap locking mechanism to our justification event? Justification before God has already taken place—an event that sustains the rest of our lives. There is nothing more to do to be saved, forever. In the final phases of Olshan's foundation reinforcement, concrete blocks are placed between the piling cap and the bottom of the sill plates. These concrete blocks are like the wise substructure that we lay in hearing and doing Jesus' words, practicing the habits we surveyed in the last chapter. These are held together by our salvation. The company still advises a moistening of the soil to maintain future performance, but they guarantee a transferable lifetime warranty! Similarly, Jesus' salvation carries an eternal lifetime warranty. The foundational truth is transferable to others as well.

Unless you choose to be a wise person, building on the Jesus-rock and laying the foundation of Jesus-embrace, you don't need to read further in this series. Yet, your choice of Jesus and His wisdom would reveal that you carefully consider the purpose of your life and will adopt the measures needed to fulfill the purpose. Reinforce the foundation. Keep moistening the soil uniformly, year-round, lifelong.

We've dealt with what comes first chronologically in intentional life-building. More so, the foundation governs the entire building process. A foundation provides the support for building buildings and building lives. The framework above and the groundwork below must be connected and compatible. A framework without the groundwork is unstable. Groundwork without the framework is unlivable. Soul Passion defines our participation in God's provision of foundation beneath as well as God's continual shaping of the framework to be built above.

Soul Passion, empowered by the bedrock on which life's foundation is anchored, permeates the entire structure. Now on to that framework, as we allow life-passion to shape our life-mission and our life-vision.

Conclusion

How can one's spiritual foundation, the Lord Jesus Christ, continue in ontological priority and increasing authority? How can He be our undergirding and overarching passion? Simplicity accompanies profundity as we answer that complex question.

If we humans only do what we value, and if what we value reveals our passions, there is only one answer to Jesus' around-the-clock, day in and day out, dawn-to-dusk authority in our lives. HE ALONE MUST BE OUR PASSION—our soul's sole passion. He must remain the nonnegotiable object of our affections, our heart's absolute desire, the final focus around which an intentional life frames its attention and forms its plans. Our focus is a Person, the Supreme Person, the only valid object of personal passion.

Is the impossible demand of loving Jesus as our first, real, true, and full love actually possible, so much so that all our other loves get loved correctly and completely? I point you to a real-life example from the world of football. (Those who play football with foot and ball are often confused by those who call that game "soccer." Most people around the world don't quite see the logic in sports nomenclature when a sport that uses an oblong leather missile, manipulated by hand after frequent committee meetings, is labeled "football.")

About a billion people watched Brazil play Germany for the 2002 FIFA World Cup Championship of accurately-labeled football. My son and I got up early to behold the finale in Seoul. After Brazil won, a few of their players dropped to their knees before the world to thank God for their victory. Various religious worldviews probably helped people interpret, even applaud, this public act, but most of them probably identified the undefined "God" whom the Brazilians thanked with their own, personal, myriad nominations for deity.

Except for Lucio—a Brazilian player who helped out the world and challenged worldviews. Every Brazilian, every South American, and every soccer fanatic knows Lucio. A wizard with his feet, he plays the number five position, which calls for near omnipresence on the field. That position demands extreme coordination, presence, offensive and defensive strategy, exertion, and execution. He needed to think both on his feet and with his feet. He critically and strategically engineered Brazil's victory.

At the postgame interview, Lucio, who fell on his knees with the praying players, clarified the identity of his God, his passionate devotion to Him in the context of his passionate pursuit of world-class football. He wore a T-shirt with large lettering that read:

JESUS

100%

My Passion

Wow! That was a testimony! But it was also a succinct and brilliant summary of passion. Football was his passion *in* life, but Jesus was the passion *of* life. There can only be one passion *of* life—your Soul Passion. And when Jesus is the 100 percent passion of your life, your other passions in life come alive, get attended to, and are excellently pursued. Upon the foundation of Soul Passion anchored to Jesus we can build and live the next levels of an Intentional Life: our life Mission and Vision!

Passion, then, clarifies our assumptions, focuses our choices, and utilizes unbroken surfaces well. A one-storied house needs floors, walls, and ceilings, just like a multi-storied one. Passion functions in that extensive, expansive, and exciting manner. It provides room while it defines limits. It furnishes assumptions and focuses choices. It enlightens and fulfills a life. The matter of passion permeates from foundation and basement up each floor to the attic and roof. Anywhere, anytime, and in any way that "matter" is used in life's building to divide, decorate, or design space, passion exists. Consequently, your love for God is the beginning, the end, and the aim of the Intentional Life. From passion flows everything else. You might as well give your passion to the only One who deserves it—God. *Let Him be the sole Soul Passion of your life.*

Every house boasts windows and doors. They open the way to let light shine in and let you look out. On pleasant nights in safe neighborhoods you swing them wide open for fresh air. You don't want to be a completely encased cavern, without entries, exits, or lights. Even a maximum-security prison allows for a door. Imagine a home without windows or doors. Unless your inside rooms are lit, you will get comfortable in the dark. Unless you let fresh air come in, you will get stuffy. All of us need windows and doors, even as we need floors, ceilings, and walls at every level. You can't live a vital life on a long-term basis in an enclosed type of situation.

Let's go beyond the enclosed, encased life into the dimensions of life where you must live intentionally. Let's continue to build the Intentional Life in Book Two—*Soul Mission*—the *ground floor* of the Intentional Life.

THE LAST WORD

These words I speak to you are not incidental additions to your life, homeowner improvements to your standard of living. They are foundational words, words to build a life on. If you work these words into your life, you are like a smart carpenter who built his house on solid rock.

—JESUS (MATT. 7:24, THE MESSAGE)

Endnotes

Chapter 1: "Gone to the Dogs!"

1. While humans normally imitate animals by unintentionally living unintentionally, we can also mimic machines during vacation—intentionally live unintentionally—away from Palm organizers and Day-Timers (cf. George Johnson, "Connoisseurs of Chaos Offer a Valuable Product: Randomness," *New York Times,* 12 June 2001, Sec. D1, 4). This trilogy discusses the distinctives of humanness, which is neither mere "animalness" nor "machineness."

2. Our culture places a high value on busyness and running in circles. The mayor of Greve, Italy, founded the Slow Cities movement (to keep up with the Slow Food movement), but too many tourists now crowd his cafes, and the city now has no time to slow down! Story by John Tagliabue, "Sometimes Slowing Down Can Really Get Hectic," *New York Times,* 7 June 2002.

3. Mark Roberts, "Home and Away," *The Economist,* 10 January 1998, 4.

4. Some biologists point to the animal urge to live, especially in higher mammals, as pointers of purpose. They have mistakenly identified *accidental* nonhuman, animal innovations with *intentional* behavior. That is, nonhuman animals have never intentionally set out on a journey or process of discovery. To paraphrase Robert Frost, humans live "accidentally, on purpose." Animals may live "purposefully, by accident."

5. A note to dog lovers: My primary illustration in this chapter arises from one puppy dog and does not stereotype animals. That comes later. It does generalize humankind. Vance Havner quipped, "I used to say civilization has gone to the dogs, but I quit saying that out of respect for dogs."

Chapter 2: An Unintentional Life

1. Quoted from *Wireless Age,* Sep–Nov 1998, 35. Cited in *Current Thoughts and Trends,* Feb 1999.

2. Compiled from *New York Times* obituaries, 3 July 1996. You may profit from an occasional reading of obituaries (especially of supposed successful people or they wouldn't have been featured) should you ask the right questions of life, any life.

3. From Christopher Lehmann-Haupt, "Icon of Psychology Has a Great Fall," *New York Times,* 13 January 1997, review of *The Creation of Dr. B: A Biography of Bruno Bettelheim,* by Richard Pollak (New York: Simon & Schuster, 1997).

4. From John Updike, *Golf Dreams: Writings on Golf* (New York: Alfred A. Knopf, 1996), reviewed by Christopher Lehmann-Haupt, "How One Small Ball Holds the Whole Universe," *New York Times,* 19 September 1996. Lehmann-Haupt explains Updike's interpretation by the intoxicating relativity that golfers experience—huge in relation to the ball, tiny in relation to the course, exactly matched to that of the other players. Updike's comment, "Many men are more faithful to their golf partners than to their wives, and have stuck with them longer," pertains best to my observations here.

5. About a dozen death clocks exist on-line. "These sites base their estimates on a brief survey of your family history and health habits. Of course, the result is no more than an educated guess. As LongToLive.com makes clear on its home page, some people 'are hit by buses.'" Pamela LiCalzi O'Connell, "Mortal Countdown," *New York Times*, 14 March 2002.

6. Holcomb B. Noble, "Dr. Viktor E. Frankl of Vienna, Psychiatrist of the Search for Meaning, Dies at 92," *New York Times*, 4 September 1997.

7. "We are going somewhere definite and destination bestows its meaning on the present mile of the journey." Hazel E. Barnes, "The Far Side of Despair," in Steven Sanders and David R. Cheney, *The Meaning of Life: Questions, Answers and Analysis* (Englewood Cliffs, N.J.: Prentice-Hall, 1980), 110.

8. "[Billy Graham's biography] makes one wonder whether the Christian calling to God is ever fully compatible with the Christian calling to family, a tension that Graham, alone among our modern fundamentalists, seems humble enough to grasp." Andrew Sullivan, "Evangelist to the World," *New York Times Book Review*, 6 July 1997, 5, in review of Billy Graham, *Just As I Am: The Autobiography of Billy Graham* (San Francisco: HarperSanFrancisco/Zondervan, 1997).

9. "Through out his writings [Sir Isaiah Berlin] insists that the great goods of human life are diverse and conflicting. They are often rivals. . . . Every choice entails a loss." John Gray, "An Idea Whose Time Won't Come," *New York Times Book Review*, 13 July 1997, 6, in review of Isaiah Berlin, *The Sense of Reality: Studies in Ideas and Their History,*" ed. Henry Hardy (New York: Farrar, Straus, & Giroux, 1997). Berlin is speaking about ultimate social values. An internal conflict clearly exists in choosing between conflicting personal values as well.

10. Philip Shenon, "Top Guns Quitting for Life at Cruising Altitude," *New York Times*, 22 October 1997, sec. A10.

11. Humankind has much in common. Mark Twain was more convinced each passing year that he and others were *alike*—that what virtues he possessed were the virtues of others, while the vices of others were all to be found in him. We could add needs, sins, desires, challenges, and wants to a list of common human traits. And so with the necessity to articulate a common supreme purpose for all human beings.

12. You will find the discussion of the benefits of supreme purpose in the Introduction to *Soul Mission*, Book Two of the Intentional Life Trilogy (due out in 2004).

13. The "emptiness of living" theme has preoccupied Western thought throughout its history. Socrates' genius established a new way of life, a new art of living with "his uncanny gift for bringing others to the brink of anxiety. In the give-and-take of a short exchange, he was able to lead his conversational partners to a recognition that although they took their lives to be incredibly important, they did not really understand what they were doing, or why, or why it was a good idea for them to be doing that rather than something else." Jonathan Lear, "The Examined Life," in Alexander Nehamas, *The Art of Living: Socratic Reflections from Plato to Foucault* (Berkeley: University of California Press, 1998) from *New York Times Book Review*, 25 October 1998, 26. "Everywhere [Socrates] looked he could find only the pretension to knowledge, not knowledge itself. In the end, Socrates recognized oracular irony: he was indeed wiser than others precisely because he understood that he lacked wisdom" (Ibid.).

14. Consequently, I shall call you later to fall on the One who is wisdom itself, to build your life on the possessor of all wisdom for life, but who exists and intervenes from outside the human paradox, irony, and quirkiness.

15. Søren Kierkegaard, *Purity of Heart Is to Will One Thing,* trans. Douglas V. Steere (New York: Harper, 1956).

Chapter 3: An Intentional Life

1. "Gillette Works Itself into a Lather When Researching Shaving Products," Roy Rivenburg, *Dallas Morning News*, 6 July 1996, sec. 3C.

2. Leon Salzman, *Treatment of the Obsessive Personality* (New York: Jason Aronson, 1980), 25. "The demands for omniscience, available only to the gods, prevent him from enjoying the rewards of limited potentialities that are available to humans" (Ibid., 25). Later, Dr. Salzman speaks about the need for grandiosity and omnipotence in obsessive behavior.

3. From tape dialogue with Mark Slouka found in his *War of the Worlds: Cyberspace and the High-tech Assault on Reality* (New York: Basic Books, 1995), 56–64.

4. Daniel Goleman, "Brain Images Show the Neural Basis of Addiction as It Is Happening," *New York Times,* 13 August 1996, sec. B5, 8.

5. Nancy Friday, *The Power of Beauty* (New York: HarperCollins, 1996).

6. James Redfield, author of *The Celestine Prophecy,* in foreword to Carol Adrienne, *The Purpose of Your Life: Finding Your Place in the World Using Synchronicity, Intuition, and Uncommon Sense* (New York: Eagle Brook, 1998), vi.

7. Adrienne, *The Purpose of Your Life,* 109.

8. Ibid., vi.

9. Q Balls are touted as the high-tech reinvention of a fortune-teller's crystal ball. You can ask any "yes" or "no" question and give it a shake. A whoosh of sounds and a swirl of lights lets you know what the Q Ball is thinking. "You never know what Q Ball will say next *('Duhhhh!')*—or which of 20 mystic advisors will say it." (Advertisement for Q Ball, *New York Times,* 12 November 1999, sec. A, 20). It is hard to imagine Q Balls becoming the synchronic authority for personal decision making, or that its answers are endowed with supernatural meaning in discerning one's future.

10. If you are willing to be saddened by and sympathetic to the inward search for "a complete life," see the serious book by Tony Schwartz, *What Really Matters: Searching for Wisdom in America* (New York.: Bantam, 1995). People courageously go to any and every plausible source to find "a complete life."

11. Written in half jest but with insight, John Tierney, "The Yellow Couch," *New York Times Magazine,* 11 August 1996, 22.

12. Adrienne, *The Purpose of Your Life,* 113.

13. Stanley L. Jaki, *The Purpose of It All* (Washington, D.C.: Regnery Gateway, 1990), ix.

Chapter 4: Profiling Passion

1. Story found in John F. Wilson, *Religion: A Preface* (Englewood Cliffs, N.J.: Prentice-Hall, 1982), 23-24.

2. The obverse is stated powerfully by Martin Luther King, Jr., who died for a cause: "If a man doesn't have anything to die for, it wasn't worth living for anyway."

3. The same raw, intentioned passion has taken a blind climber up Mount Everest when "a majority of the people have difficulty even getting to the base camp, let alone the summit." He lost his sight at age 13 and began climbing three years later. At 32, he scaled Everest "by following the sound of bells tied to the jackets of his climbing mates and Sherpa guides." (From Associated Press article, "Oldest, First Blind Climber Reach the Summit of Everest," *Dallas Morning News,* 26 May 2001, 28A.)

4. A more biblical treatment of *passion* arises later in chapter 7, "Soul Passion, Sole Passion."

5. R. L. Ottley, "Passivity," *Encyclopedia of Religion and Ethics,* vol. IX, ed. James Hastings (New York: Charles Scribner, 1951), 659.

6. Sidney Low wrote: "Englishmen, in politics, get on quite comfortably without a Weltanschauung [or worldview]. Germans require it for daily use" (brackets mine). *Edinburgh Review* (October 1914), 272. Cited by C. J. Cadoux, *The Christian Crusade: A Study in the Supreme Purpose of Life* (London: J. M. Dent & Sons, 1924), 3. Cadoux notes that the need for a worldview "is true in other things besides politics."

7. H. H. Esser, "Creation, Foundation, Creature, Maker," *Dictionary of New Testament Theology* [DNNT], 4 vols., Gen. ed. Colin Brown (Grand Rapids: Regency Reference Library, 1986), I:376. It is interesting that the classical use of the verb *kataballo* ("throw down") means to "bring from an upright into a horizontal position" (Ibid.). That's what the Founder-Creator did to the creature in the Fall. The Creator also laid (threw and stacked the stones into the foundation trench) the foundation by which mankind can be rebuilt.

8. In classical Greek, "foundation" could refer to the literal stones beneath a building. In a legal sense it "describe[s] the right to possession of a building, or in philosophical thought, where the term means the basis of a system (from *"qemelios" [themelios]* by J. Blunck, DNTT, I:660–2). A third word, *hedraio(s)(ma)*, occurs four times as a synonym of themelios.

9. H. Schönweiss, "Firm, Foundation, Certainty, Confirm," *DNTT,* I:658.

10. From a financial standpoint, *katabole* can mean payment (laying out) of certain sums of money. A redemption nuance is evident there. Biologically, the word denotes the depositing of seed in the ground. That seed-deposit carries a "new birth" nuance. Jesus is not a mere, shiny, symbolic foundation stone unveiled at building dedications. He buys you and births you and lays strong the claim to become your new foundation.

11. Paul also writes about the foundation of the apostles and prophets with Jesus as chief cornerstone, bringing reconciliation between those far off, and consummation to God's spiritual building program—the universal church (Eph. 2:20).

12. Hebrews 6:1 refers to the foundation of repentance from acts that lead to death. This foundation only needs to be laid once and is the flip side of faith in God. Repentance and faith in Jesus alone are the two sides of the salvation-foundation which must be laid to begin reconstructing your life.

13. In an interesting twist to the metaphor, Peter sees the foundation stone which unbelievers reject becoming their stumbling block (1 Peter 2:6–8). Jesus is either your stratum rock of salvation or stumbling block of condemnation.

14. New Testament metaphors refer to Jesus as the foundation for not being moved, shaken, or overwhelmed by "the gates of Hades" (Matt. 16:18); flood conditions (Luke 17:26–31); nor the future "assessment" day (1 Cor. 3:10–13).

15. Barry James, "Lessons of History in Bubble Madness: Speculative Follies Have Long Past," *International Herald Tribune,* 3–4 October 1998, 24.

Chapter 5: Reinforcing Passion

1. Much contemporary spirituality calls for us to look inside ourselves rather than reaching out to "a Being" for spiritual foundations. While attractive, that counsel is unwise. You can go as deep as possible into an unsettled life but you will not find an adequate foundation. If you place nickels in your pocket, you can't find dimes there, however much you dig, however many times you try, and however long you take. We need an internal, spiritual foundation, but it is not sourced inside ourselves.

2. Now you know from whom I borrowed the dominant metaphor for this series—life as a building!

3. "The Season of El Niño," *The Economist,* 9 May 1998, 35–38.

4. Editorial page, "In Praise of Knowledge," *The Economist,* 27 May 1995, 20.

5. David Goodstein, "Mathematics to Madness, and Back," review of *A Beautiful Mind,* by Sylvia Nasar (New York: Simon & Schuster, 1998), *New York Times,* 11 June 1998, sec. B10.

6. A. B. Bruce, "The Synoptic Gospels," *Expositor's Greek Testament,* ed. W. Robertson Nicoll (Grand Rapids: Eerdmans, 1976), 135.

7. W. T. Dayton, "Folly," *Zondervan Pictorial Encyclopedia of the Bible,* eds. Merrill C. Tenney and Steven Barabas, Vol. 1 (Grand Rapids: Zondervan, 1976), 581.

8. The tower, which was started in the late twelfth century as a point of pride for the mighty seafaring people of Pisa, began leaning almost immediately as the foundation of the 14,500-ton monument shifted in the sandy soil (from "'Pisa Party' Town to Give Tower's Recast Tilt a Whirl," *Dallas Morning News,* 17 June 2001, sec. A26).

9. A. T. Robertson, *Word Pictures in the New Testament,* vol. 1 (Nashville: Broadman, 1930), 63.

10. Matthew 7:21–22 notes that some who verbalized and publicized the lordship of Jesus by grand words and miracles will not in fact enter the kingdom of heaven. I don't take this passage on Jesus' lordship to show criteria for entry into salvation. It could be simply a statement of respect, though in Matthew's context Jesus is claiming messianic (and probably divine) authority in eschatological terms. The repetition "Lord, Lord" was Semitically emphatic denoting a higher messianic meaning

than simply "master." Apparently, many will say, "Lord, Lord," but only some will enter the kingdom of heaven. It is a differentiation between the foolish and wise who *both* say, "Lord, Lord," to Him. The wise hear the words of Jesus, the exclusive Lord, over against the traditional teaching (cf. vv. 27, 31), *and* practice them. The foolish hear but don't practice His words. One can profess the "lordship" of Jesus and yet be unwise. Practicing the truth makes us wise in our life-building, and we shall be blessed (James 1:21–25). "Those who pretend to have faith, who have a merely intellectual commitment, or who enjoy Jesus in small doses are foolish builders. When the storms of life come, their structures fool no one, above all not God (cf. Ezek. 13:10–16)." D. A. Carson, "Matthew," *Expositor's Bible Commentary* (Grand Rapids: Zondervan, 1995), 8:194.

11. For the "hearing and doing" theme, see Mark 4:20; Luke 8:21 and 11:28.

Chapter 6: Connecting Passion

1. Wayne Rice, *More Hot Illustrations for Youth Talks* (Grand Rapids: Zondervan, 1995), 160.

2. Values guide actions so much that a hospice director recommends creating an ethical will for posterity as a means of defining and passing along values to loved ones. Cf. www.ethicalwill.com hosted by Barry Baines. Also see Rabbi Jack Riemer and Nathaniel Stampfer, *So That Your Values Live On—Ethical Wills and How to Prepare Them* (Woodstock, Vt.: Jewish Lights Publishing, 1991).

3. Stephen R. Covey, *The Seven Habits of Highly Effective People* (New York: Simon & Schuster, 1989), 72.

4. Values may be subjectively or objectively valuable. To keep from personal and human arbitrariness, we will look at who (or what) is ultimately and absolutely valuable (objective) and important to us (subjective). We, of course, do not make an object valuable in itself. We can only make it valuable for us.

5. The term "well-feeling" is suggested by Vincent Colapietro to "cover subjective states of pleasure, enjoyment, positive moods, positive attitudes, satisfaction, contentment, peace of mind, and so on." Quoted in Deal W. Hudson, *Happiness and the Limits of Satisfaction* (Lanham, Md.: Rowman & Littlefield, 1996), xx, n. 1.

6. "Well-being includes the possession of moral goodness, but may also include non-moral goods or may extend to global appraisals of an individual life." Ibid.

7. I spell "holism" with a "w" to differentiate it from "New Age" connotations and other religious inclinations of contemporary spirituality.

8. Matthew 5:11–12 expands the final Beatitude into second person direct address and makes an implicit claim for Jesus as God. Jesus' disciples are to face persecution even as the prophets of God did.

9. If you're stuck, here's a little help. I see the foundational value of Matthew 5:10 as *sacrifice* or *endurance* extending all the way to persecution. If you are going to practice the values of the earlier verses, you shouldn't be surprised by persecution from counter-kingdom animosity. The application could relate to "standing alone for Christ regardless of cost, having counted the cost." Obedience might mean checking for areas of public compromise or increasing lawlessness, and addressing them in a *public* way.

10. In this note, I share another series of equations that sets out my philosophy of the "knowing" and "doing" aspects of the wise, transformed life. Read slower still!
Inspiration and (+) information without (–) application equals (=) frustration
Information – inspiration = boredom
Information – application = constipation
Inspiration – information = shallowness
Inspiration – application = desperation
Application – information = legalism
Application – inspiration = apathy
Inspiration + information + application = transformation

11. D. A. Carson, "Matthew," *Expositor's Bible Commentary* (Grand Rapids: Zondervan, 1995), 8:194.

Chapter 7: Soul Passion, Sole Passion

1. Bernard of Clairvaux, *The Love of God* (Portland, Ore.: Multnomah, 1983).

2. Dallas Willard, *Renovation of the Heart* (Colorado Springs, Colo.: NavPress, 2002), 30. Willard notes six basic aspects of the whole person that interplay to make up "human nature": thought, feeling, choice, body, social context, soul.

3. Jonathan Edwards, *The Works of Jonathan Edwards,* ed. Perry Miller, 5 vols. (New Haven: Yale University Press, 1959). See vol. 2, the source for this set of citations where "love" is one of several scriptural affections. The heart is the seat of all these affections. Edwards is sometimes referred to as the "Theologian of the Heart." (See Harold Simonson, *Jonathan Edwards: Theologian of the Heart* [Grand Rapids: Eerdmans, 1974].)

4. The related Hebrew terms are: *nephesh; l?b; l?b?b; ruach.* See "Soul," *New Bible Dictionary* (Wheaton, Ill.: Tyndale, 1962).

5. I borrow this valuable insight from Edward Collins Vacek, S.J., *Love, Human and Divine: The Heart of Christian Ethics* (Washington, D.C.: Georgetown University Press, 1994). The best recent study on Christian love, we find this treatment in his section on "Correlative Objective Values," 16ff.

6. Ibid., 18.

7. Lawrence O. Richards, "Mind," *Expository Dictionary of Bible Words* (Grand Rapids: Regency Reference Library, 1985), 442.

8. Quoting Richard Foster, *Devotional Classics: Selected Readings for Individuals and Groups,* eds. Richard J. Foster and James Bryan Smith (San Francisco: HarperSanFrancisco, 1990), 24.

9. C. S. Lewis, *Mere Christianity* (New York: Macmillan, rev. ed. 1952), 74.

10. Again, in older Bible versions (the Authorized Version and *Revised Version*), Acts 1:3 reads, "to whom he also showed himself after his passion." The newer versions translate the word as "suffering."

11. When "passion" began to refer to powerful emotion, unflinching pursuit, "over-emotion that robs a man of his self-control, . . . he exhibited 'pathos' in inordinate and inappropriate ways (cf. 'pathos' in Rom 1:26; Col 3:5; 1 Thess 4:5)." Burton Scott Easton, "Passion," *International Standard Bible Encyclopedia* (Grand Rapids: Eerdmans, 1939), IV:2256.

12. Again see the article on "Passivity" by R. L. Ottley, in *Encyclopedia of Religion and Ethics,* ed. James Hastings (New York: Charles Scribner, 1951), vol. IX:659–61.

13. Vacek, *Love, Human and Divine,* 5. He continues, "These affections give rise to both doctrine and practice. Ultimately our perfection as a person is measured strictly according to the degree of development of our loves."

14. *George Macdonald, An Anthology,* ed. C. S. Lewis (New York: Macmillan, 1978), 23.

15. An entire theology of neighborly love—love of aliens and doing good to the stranger—pervade the Old Testament (e.g., Rahab and the spies), is proven in Jesus' parables (e.g., the Good Samaritan) and miracles (e.g., the Syrophoenician woman), and is completed by New Testament injunctions (Gal. 6:10) and example (Acts 10; 15). "Neighbor" extends from bosom lover, to personal friend, to foreigner, even to enemy.

16. Oswald Chambers, *My Utmost for His Highest,* ed. James Reiman (Grand Rapids: Discovery House, 1992), June 2. I identify this book by date rather than page number hence.

Chapter 8: Nurturing Passion

1. We are moving from what it takes to be justified before God—by grace alone through faith alone in Jesus Christ alone—to what it means to be a Christian—laying a foundation of wise obedience to Christ.

2. One of my esteemed mentors, Fred Smith Sr., uses another metaphor from building construction to understand the role of spiritual disciplines, that of "scaffolding." To confuse the scaffolding

with the building is to focus erroneously. Since the building of our lives is never finished, the scaffolding stays year-round, lifelong. However, the building is not the scaffolding. Spirituality itself is not the spiritual discipline.

A supporting concept in construction is *centering*: "Temporary construction to support arches and similar structures while the mortar or concrete is setting or the steel is being joined. As soon as the work is set, the centering is carefully removed; this process is called 'striking the cent[e]ring.' . . . The same term is applied to the use of scaffold boards to support concrete floors while they are hardening." Taken from "Falsework," *Encyclopaedia Britannica 2002,* expanded DVD (Chicago: Brittanica Centre, 2002). There is a correlation: spiritual disciplines enable spirituality temporarily and is not a true work!

3. Johannes P. Louw and Eugene A. Nida, "Gumnazo," *Greek-English Lexicon of the New Testament based on Semantic Domains* (New York: United Bible Societies, 1988, 1989), 36:11 and 88:8.

4. Oswald Chambers, *My Utmost for His Highest,* ed. James Reiman (Grand Rapids: Discovery House, 1992), May 12.

5. Klaus Issler effectively explores "friendship with God" as the core of the spiritual life in *Wasting Time with God: A Christian Spirituality of Friendship with God* (Downers Grove, Ill.: InterVarsity, 2001).

6. Fine evangelical authors on both the theology and practice of disciplines include Richard Foster, *Celebration of Discipline: The Path to Spiritual Growth* (San Francisco: Harper & Row, 1988); Douglas J. Rumford, *Soul Shaping* (Wheaton, Ill.: Tyndale, 1996); and Dallas Willard, *The Spirit of the Disciplines* (San Francisco: Harper & Row, 1988).

7. Indeed, I see the four kinds of disciplines fitting under the four love-nouns of the Great Commandment: Heart—attachment; Soul—detachment; Mind—alignment; Strength—engagement.

8. Chambers, *My Utmost for His Highest,* March 4.

9. A relevant technical comment parallels our treatment of passion: "From the vantage of Christology, our individual quests for meaning, across the wildly diverse circumstances of life, are still united in Christ. Christ remains the *telos* that subsumes humanity's striving after meaning." William A. Dembski, "Christology and Human Development" in *Foundations,* Winter 1997, 5:1:14.

About the Author

Dr. Ramesh Richard is a professor at Dallas Theological Seminary, where he teaches expository preaching, the spiritual life, and worldview apologetics. He is also the founder and president of *RREACH* International, through which God has permitted him to serve as a global spokesman for the Lord Jesus Christ.

RREACH is an acronym for Ramesh Richard Evangelism and Church Helps. A global proclamation ministry, the vision of *RREACH* is to change the way *one billion individuals* think and hear about the Lord Jesus Christ. Its mission is to "proclaim the Lord Jesus Christ worldwide, with a strategic burden for strengthening the pastoral leaders and evangelizing the opinion leaders of weaker economies."

From his platform at *RREACH*, Dr. Richard travels throughout the world, clarifying the message of the Bible. His audiences are wide-ranging—from non-Christian intellectuals at Harvard University to poor pastors in Haiti, from gatherings of a few to a hundred thousand. In recent years he has been speaking to crowds of men about their spiritual responsibilities in stadiums across the United States. The Lord has given him the opportunity to train thousands of church leaders in more than seventy countries to preach, live, and think biblically. He also has the privilege of exposing society's "opinion leaders" to the Lord Jesus Christ. Each New Year's Day he presents the gospel on prime-time, secular television to large numbers of English-speaking, internet-active audiences in about one hundred countries.

A theologian, philosopher, evangelist, and author, Dr. Richard holds a Th.D. in Systematic Theology from Dallas Theological Seminary, and a Ph.D. in Philosophy from the University of Delhi.

He lives in the Dallas, Texas, area with his wife, Bonnie, their children, Ryan, Robby, and Sitara.

Order Dr. Ramesh Richard's

"Life Rocks"

DVD/Video summary of

THE INTENTIONAL LIFE

from RREACH International
www.rreach.org

5500 West Plano Parkway, Suite 100, Plano, TX 75093
Telephone: 972-733-3402; Fax 972-733-3495;
Email: info@rreach.org

Since 1894, Moody Publishers has been dedicated to equip and motivate people to advance the cause of Christ by publishing evangelical Christian literature and other media for all ages, around the world. Because we are a ministry of the Moody Bible Institute of Chicago, a portion of the proceeds from the sale of this book go to train the next generation of Christian leaders.

If we may serve you in any way in your spiritual journey toward understanding Christ and the Christian life, please contact us at www.moodypublishers.com.

"All Scripture is God-breathed and is useful for teaching, rebuking, correcting and training in righteousness, so that the man of God may be thoroughly equipped for every good work."
—2 TIMOTHY 3:16, 17

MOODY
PUBLISHERS

THE NAME YOU CAN TRUST®

SOUL PASSION TEAM

ACQUIRING EDITOR:
Greg Thornton

COPY EDITOR:
Neil Wilson, Livingstone Corporation

COVER DESIGN:
UDG Design Works

INTERIOR DESIGN:
Livingstone Corporation

PRINTING AND BINDING:
Quebecor World Book Services